HBR's 10 Must Reads

UPDATED & EXPANDED

Change Management

HBR's 10 Must Reads

HBR's 10 Must Reads are definitive collections of classic ideas, practical advice, and essential thinking from the pages of *Harvard Business Review*. Exploring topics like disruptive innovation, emotional intelligence, and new technology in our ever-evolving world, these books empower any leader to make bold decisions and inspire others.

TITLES INCLUDE:

- HBR's 10 Must Reads for New Managers
- HBR's 10 Must Reads on AI
- HBR's 10 Must Reads on Building a Great Culture
- HBR's 10 Must Reads on Change Management
- HBR's 10 Must Reads on Communication
- HBR's 10 Must Reads on Data Strategy
- HBR's 10 Must Reads on Decision-Making
- HBR's 10 Must Reads on Design Thinking
- HBR's 10 Must Reads on Digital Transformation
- HBR's 10 Must Reads on Emotional Intelligence
- HBR's 10 Must Reads on High Performance
- HBR's 10 Must Reads on Innovation
- HBR's 10 Must Reads on Leadership
- HBR's 10 Must Reads on Leading Winning Teams
- HBR's 10 Must Reads on Managing People
- HBR's 10 Must Reads on Managing Yourself
- HBR's 10 Must Reads on Marketing
- HBR's 10 Must Reads on Mental Toughness
- HBR's 10 Must Reads on Strategy
- HBR's 10 Must Reads on Women and Leadership
- HBR's 10 Must Reads Boxed Set (6 Books)
- HBR's 10 Must Reads Ultimate Boxed Set (14 Books)

For a full list, visit hbr.org/mustreads.

UPDATED & EXPANDED
_____

Change Management

Harvard Business Review Press
Boston, Massachusetts

HBR Press Quantity Sales Discounts

Harvard Business Review Press titles are available at significant quantity discounts when purchased in bulk for leadership development programs, client gifts, or sales promotions. Opportunities to co-brand copies with your logo or messaging are also available. For details and discount information for both print and ebook formats, contact booksales@hbr.org or visit www.hbr.org/bulksales.

Copyright 2025 Harvard Business School Publishing Corporation

All rights reserved

Printed in the United States of America

10 9 8 7 6 5 4 3 2 1

No part of this publication may be reproduced, stored in or introduced into a retrieval system, or transmitted, in any form, or by any means (electronic, mechanical, photocopying, recording, or otherwise), without the prior permission of the publisher. Requests for permission should be directed to permissions@harvardbusiness.org or mailed to Permissions, Harvard Business School Publishing, 60 Harvard Way, Boston, Massachusetts 02163.

The web addresses referenced in this book were live and correct at the time of the book's publication but may be subject to change.

Cataloging-in-Publication data is forthcoming.

ISBN: 979-8-89279-176-2
eISBN: 979-8-89279-177-9

The paper used in this publication meets the requirements of the American National Standard for Permanence of Paper for Publications and Documents in Libraries and Archives Z39.48-1992.

Contents

1 Leading Change: Why Transformation Efforts Fail   1
Eight steps can help companies avoid common mistakes.

by John P. Kotter

2 Transformations That Work   19
Lessons from organizations that have defied the odds.

by Michael Mankins and Patrick Litre

QUICK READ

Let Go of What Made Your Company Great   35
To succeed in the future, selectively forget the past.

by Vijay Govindarajan

3 Persuade Your Company to Change Before It's Too Late   41
Making the case when the evidence isn't clear.

by Pontus M. A. Siren, Scott D. Anthony, and Utsav Bhatt

4 Getting Reorgs Right   55
A practical guide to a misunderstood—and often mismanaged—process.

by Stephen Heidari-Robinson and Suzanne Heywood

QUICK READ

Six Steps for Gaining Employee Buy-In 67
Create a culture that embraces the new.

by Andrea Belk Olson

5 Storytelling That Drives Bold Change 73
Craft a narrative that honors the past and charts a path forward.

by Frances X. Frei and Anne Morriss

QUICK READ

Organize Your Transformation Around Purpose and Benefits 89
Employees need to know what's in it for them.

by Antonio Nieto-Rodriguez

6 The Network Secrets of Great Change Agents 101
These leaders share three key attributes.

by Julie Battilana and Tiziana Casciaro

7 What Everyone Gets Wrong About Change Management 115
Poor execution is only one part of the problem.

by N. Anand and Jean-Louis Barsoux

8 A Survival Guide for Leaders 135
Tactics for staving off challenges and doubts.

by Ronald Heifetz and Marty Linsky

9 The Real Reason People Won't Change 159
Understand "competing commitment"—and what to do about it.

by Robert Kegan and Lisa Lahey

10 Your Workforce Is More Adaptable Than You Think 179
Retraining can be a competitive advantage.

by Joseph Fuller, Judith K. Wallenstein, Manjari Raman, and Alice de Chalendar

Discussion Guide	193
About the Contributors	197
Index	203

UPDATED & EXPANDED

Change Management

Leading Change: Why Transformation Efforts Fail

by John P. Kotter

Over the past decade, I have watched more than 100 companies try to remake themselves into significantly better competitors. They have included large organizations (Ford) and small ones (Landmark Communications), companies based in the United States (General Motors) and elsewhere (British Airways), corporations that were on their knees (Eastern Airlines), and companies that were earning good money (Bristol-Myers Squibb). These efforts have gone under many banners: total quality management, reengineering, right sizing, restructuring, cultural change, and turnaround. But, in almost every case, the basic goal has been the same: to make fundamental changes in how business is conducted in order to help cope with a new, more challenging market environment.

A few of these corporate change efforts have been very successful. A few have been utter failures. Most fall somewhere in between, with a distinct tilt toward the lower end of the scale. The lessons that can be drawn are interesting and will probably be relevant to even more organizations in the increasingly competitive business environment of the coming decade.

The most general lesson to be learned from the more successful cases is that the change process goes through a series of phases that, in total, usually require a considerable length of time. Skipping steps creates only the illusion of speed and never produces a satisfying result. A second very general lesson is that critical mistakes in any of the phases can have a devastating impact, slowing momentum and negating hard-won gains. Perhaps because we have relatively little experience in renewing organizations, even very capable people often make at least one big error.

Error 1: Not Establishing a Great Enough Sense of Urgency

Most successful change efforts begin when some individuals or some groups start to look hard at a company's competitive situation, market position, technological trends, and financial performance. They focus on the potential revenue drop when an important patent expires, the five-year trend in declining margins in a core business, or an emerging market that everyone seems to be ignoring. They then find ways to communicate this information broadly and dramatically, especially with respect to crises, potential crises, or great opportunities that are very timely. This first step is essential because just getting a transformation program started requires the aggressive cooperation

Idea in Brief

Most major change initiatives—whether intended to boost quality, improve culture, or reverse a corporate death spiral—generate only lukewarm results. Many fail miserably.

Why? Kotter maintains that too many managers don't realize transformation is a process, not an event. It advances through stages that build on each other. And it takes years. Pressured to accelerate the process, managers skip stages. But shortcuts never work.

Equally troubling, even highly capable managers make critical mistakes—such as declaring victory too soon. Result? Loss of momentum, reversal of hard-won gains, and devastation of the entire transformation effort.

By understanding the stages of change—and the pitfalls unique to each stage—you boost your chances of a successful transformation. The payoff? Your organization flexes with tectonic shifts in competitors, markets, and technologies—leaving rivals far behind.

---

of many individuals. Without motivation, people won't help and the effort goes nowhere.

Compared with other steps in the change process, phase one can sound easy. It is not. Well over 50% of the companies I have watched fail in this first phase. What are the reasons for that failure? Sometimes executives underestimate how hard it can be to drive people out of their comfort zones. Sometimes they grossly overestimate how successful they have already been in increasing urgency. Sometimes they lack patience: "Enough with the preliminaries; let's get on with it." In many cases, executives become paralyzed by the downside possibilities. They worry that employees with seniority will become defensive, that morale will drop, that events will spin out of control, that short-term business results will be jeopardized, that the stock will sink, and that they will be blamed for creating a crisis.

A paralyzed senior management often comes from having too many managers and not enough leaders. Management's mandate is to minimize risk and to keep the current system operating.

Eight Steps to Transforming Your Organization

1. Establishing a sense of urgency
   - Examining market and competitive realities
   - Identifying and discussing crises, potential crises, or major opportunities
2. Forming a powerful guiding coalition
   - Assembling a group with enough power to lead the change effort
   - Encouraging the group to work together as a team
3. Creating a vision
   - Creating a vision to help direct the change effort
   - Developing strategies for achieving that vision
4. Communicating the vision
   - Using every vehicle possible to communicate the new vision and strategies
   - Teaching new behaviors by the example of the guiding coalition
5. Empowering others to act on the vision
   - Getting rid of obstacles to change

Change, by definition, requires creating a new system, which in turn always demands leadership. Phase one in a renewal process typically goes nowhere until enough real leaders are promoted or hired into senior-level jobs.

Transformations often begin, and begin well, when an organization has a new head who is a good leader and who sees the need for a major change. If the renewal target is the entire company, the

- Changing systems or structures that seriously undermine the vision
- Encouraging risk-taking and nontraditional ideas, activities, and actions

6. Planning for and creating short-term wins
   - Planning for visible performance improvements
   - Creating those improvements
   - Recognizing and rewarding employees involved in the improvements

7. Consolidating improvements and producing still more change
   - Using increased credibility to change systems, structures, and policies that don't fit the vision
   - Hiring, promoting, and developing employees who can implement the vision
   - Reinvigorating the process with new projects, themes, and change agents

8. Institutionalizing new approaches
   - Articulating the connections between the new behaviors and corporate success
   - Developing the means to ensure leadership development and succession

---

CEO is key. If change is needed in a division, the division general manager is key. When these individuals are not new leaders, great leaders, or change champions, phase one can be a huge challenge.

Bad business results are both a blessing and a curse in the first phase. On the positive side, losing money does catch people's attention. But it also gives less maneuvering room. With good business results, the opposite is true: convincing people of the need for change is much harder, but you have more resources to help make changes.

But whether the starting point is good performance or bad, in the more successful cases I have witnessed, an individual or a group always facilitates a frank discussion of potentially unpleasant facts: about new competition, shrinking margins, decreasing market share, flat earnings, a lack of revenue growth, or other relevant indices of a declining competitive position. Because there seems to be an almost universal human tendency to shoot the bearer of bad news, especially if the head of the organization is not a change champion, executives in these companies often rely on outsiders to bring unwanted information. Wall Street analysts, customers, and consultants can all be helpful in this regard. The purpose of all this activity, in the words of one former CEO of a large European company, is "to make the status quo seem more dangerous than launching into the unknown."

In a few of the most successful cases, a group has manufactured a crisis. One CEO deliberately engineered the largest accounting loss in the company's history, creating huge pressures from Wall Street in the process. One division president commissioned first-ever customer-satisfaction surveys, knowing full well that the results would be terrible. He then made these findings public. On the surface, such moves can look unduly risky. But there is also risk in playing it too safe: when the urgency rate is not pumped up enough, the transformation process cannot succeed and the long-term future of the organization is put in jeopardy.

When is the urgency rate high enough? From what I have seen, the answer is when about 75% of a company's management is honestly convinced that business-as-usual is totally unacceptable. Anything less can produce very serious problems later on in the process.

Error 2: Not Creating a Powerful Enough Guiding Coalition

Major renewal programs often start with just one or two people. In cases of successful transformation efforts, the leadership coalition grows and grows over time. But whenever some minimum mass is not achieved early in the effort, nothing much worthwhile happens.

It is often said that major change is impossible unless the head of the organization is an active supporter. What I am talking about goes far beyond that. In successful transformations, the chairman or president or division general manager, plus another 5 or 15 or 50 people, come together and develop a shared commitment to excellent performance through renewal. In my experience, this group never includes all of the company's most senior executives because some people just won't buy in, at least not at first. But in the most successful cases, the coalition is always pretty powerful—in terms of titles, information and expertise, reputations and relationships.

In both small and large organizations, a successful guiding team may consist of only three to five people during the first year of a renewal effort. But in big companies, the coalition needs to grow to the 20 to 50 range before much progress can be made in phase three and beyond. Senior managers always form the core of the group. But sometimes you find board members, a representative from a key customer, or even a powerful union leader.

Because the guiding coalition includes members who are not part of senior management, it tends to operate outside of the normal hierarchy by definition. This can be awkward, but it is clearly necessary. If the existing hierarchy were working well, there would be no need for a major transformation. But since the current system is not working, reform generally demands activity outside of formal boundaries, expectations, and protocol.

A high sense of urgency within the managerial ranks helps enormously in putting a guiding coalition together. But more is usually required. Someone needs to get these people together, help them develop a shared assessment of their company's problems and opportunities, and create a minimum level of trust and communication. Off-site retreats, for two or three days, are one popular vehicle for accomplishing this task. I have seen many groups of 5 to 35 executives attend a series of these retreats over a period of months.

Companies that fail in phase two usually underestimate the difficulties of producing change and thus the importance of a powerful guiding coalition. Sometimes they have no history of teamwork at the top and therefore undervalue the importance of this type of coalition. Sometimes they expect the team to be led by a staff executive from human resources, quality, or strategic planning instead of a key line manager. No matter how capable or dedicated the staff head, groups without strong line leadership never achieve the power that is required.

Efforts that don't have a powerful enough guiding coalition can make apparent progress for a while. But, sooner or later, the opposition gathers itself together and stops the change.

Error 3: Lacking a Vision

In every successful transformation effort that I have seen, the guiding coalition develops a picture of the future that is relatively easy to communicate and appeals to customers, stockholders, and employees. A vision always goes beyond the numbers that are typically found in five-year plans. A vision says something that helps clarify the direction in which an organization needs to move. Sometimes the first draft comes mostly from a single individual. It is usually a bit blurry, at least initially. But after the coalition works at it for 3 or 5 or even 12 months, something much better emerges through their tough analytical thinking and a little dreaming. Eventually, a strategy for achieving that vision is also developed.

In one midsize European company, the first pass at a vision contained two-thirds of the basic ideas that were in the final product. The concept of global reach was in the initial version from the beginning. So was the idea of becoming preeminent in certain businesses. But one central idea in the final version—getting out of low value-added activities—came only after a series of discussions over a period of several months.

Without a sensible vision, a transformation effort can easily dissolve into a list of confusing and incompatible projects that can take the organization in the wrong direction or nowhere at all. Without a sound vision, the reengineering project in the accounting department, the new 360-degree performance appraisal from the human resources department, the plant's quality program, the cultural change project in the sales force will not add up in a meaningful way.

In failed transformations, you often find plenty of plans and directives and programs, but no vision. In one case, a company gave out four-inch-thick notebooks describing its change effort. In mind-numbing detail, the books spelled out procedures, goals, methods, and deadlines. But nowhere was there a clear and compelling statement of where all this was leading. Not surprisingly, most of the employees with whom I talked were either confused or alienated. The big, thick books did not rally them together or inspire change. In fact, they probably had just the opposite effect.

In a few of the less successful cases that I have seen, management had a sense of direction, but it was too complicated or blurry to be useful. Recently, I asked an executive in a midsize company to describe his vision and received in return a barely comprehensible 30-minute lecture. Buried in his answer were the basic elements of a sound vision. But they were buried—deeply.

A useful rule of thumb: if you can't communicate the vision to someone in five minutes or less and get a reaction that signifies both understanding and interest, you are not yet done with this phase of the transformation process.

Error 4: Undercommunicating the Vision by a Factor of Ten

I've seen three patterns with respect to communication, all very common. In the first, a group actually does develop a pretty good transformation vision and then proceeds to communicate it by holding a single meeting or sending out a single communication. Having used about 0.0001% of the yearly intracompany communication, the group is startled that few people seem to understand the new approach. In the second pattern, the head of the organization spends a considerable amount of time making speeches to employee groups, but most people still don't get it (not surprising, since vision captures only 0.0005% of the total yearly communication). In the third pattern, much more effort goes into newsletters and speeches, but some very visible senior executives still behave in ways that are antithetical to the vision. The net result is that cynicism among the troops goes up, while belief in the communication goes down.

Transformation is impossible unless hundreds or thousands of people are willing to help, often to the point of making short-term sacrifices. Employees will not make sacrifices, even if they are unhappy with the status quo, unless they believe that useful change is possible. Without credible communication, and a lot of it, the hearts and minds of the troops are never captured.

This fourth phase is particularly challenging if the short-term sacrifices include job losses. Gaining understanding and support is tough when downsizing is a part of the vision. For this reason, successful visions usually include new growth possibilities and the commitment to treat fairly anyone who is laid off.

Executives who communicate well incorporate messages into their hour-by-hour activities. In a routine discussion about a business problem, they talk about how proposed solutions fit (or don't fit) into the bigger picture. In a regular performance appraisal, they talk about how the employee's behavior helps or undermines the vision. In a review of a division's quarterly performance, they talk not only about the numbers but also about how the division's executives are contributing to the transformation. In a routine Q&A with employees at a company facility, they tie their answers back to renewal goals.

In more successful transformation efforts, executives use all existing communication channels to broadcast the vision. They turn boring and unread company newsletters into lively articles about the vision. They take ritualistic and tedious quarterly management meetings and turn them into exciting discussions of the transformation. They throw out much of the company's generic management education and replace it with courses that focus on business problems and the new vision. The guiding principle is simple: use every possible channel, especially those that are being wasted on nonessential information.

Perhaps even more important, most of the executives I have known in successful cases of major change learn to "walk the talk." They consciously attempt to become a living symbol of the new corporate culture. This is often not easy. A 60-year-old plant manager who has spent precious little time over 40 years thinking about customers will not suddenly behave in a customer-oriented way. But I have witnessed just such a person change, and change a great deal. In that case, a high level of urgency helped. The fact that the man was a part of the guiding coalition and the vision-creation team also helped. So did all the communication, which kept reminding him of the desired behavior, and all the feedback from his peers and subordinates, which helped him see when he was not engaging in that behavior.

Communication comes in both words and deeds, and the latter are often the most powerful form. Nothing undermines change more than behavior by important individuals that is inconsistent with their words.

Error 5: Not Removing Obstacles to the New Vision

Successful transformations begin to involve large numbers of people as the process progresses. Employees are emboldened to try new approaches, to develop new ideas, and to provide leadership. The only constraint is that the actions fit within the broad parameters of the overall vision. The more people involved, the better the outcome.

To some degree, a guiding coalition empowers others to take action simply by successfully communicating the new direction. But communication is never sufficient by itself. Renewal also requires the removal of obstacles. Too often, an employee understands the new vision and wants to help make it happen. But an elephant appears to be blocking the path. In some cases, the elephant is in the person's head, and the challenge is to convince the individual that no external obstacle exists. But in most cases, the blockers are very real.

Sometimes the obstacle is the organizational structure: narrow job categories can seriously undermine efforts to increase productivity or make it very difficult even to think about customers. Sometimes compensation or performance-appraisal systems make people choose between the new vision and their own self-interest. Perhaps worst of all are bosses who refuse to change and who make demands that are inconsistent with the overall effort.

One company began its transformation process with much publicity and actually made good progress through the fourth phase. Then the change effort ground to a halt because the officer in charge of the company's largest division was allowed to undermine most of the new initiatives. He paid lip service to the process but did not change his behavior or encourage his managers to change. He did not reward the unconventional ideas called for in the vision. He allowed human resource systems to remain intact even when they were clearly inconsistent with the new ideals. I think the officer's motives were complex. To some degree, he did not believe the company needed major change. To some degree, he felt personally threatened by all the change. To some degree, he was afraid that he could not produce both change and the expected operating profit. But despite the fact that they backed the renewal effort, the other officers did virtually nothing to stop the one blocker. Again, the reasons were complex. The company had no history of confronting problems like this. Some people were afraid of the officer. The CEO was concerned that he might lose a talented executive. The net result was disastrous. Lower-level managers concluded that senior management had lied to them about their commitment to renewal, cynicism grew, and the whole effort collapsed.

In the first half of a transformation, no organization has the momentum, power, or time to get rid of all obstacles. But the big ones must be confronted and removed. If the blocker is a person, it is important that they be treated fairly and in a way that is consistent with the new vision. But action is essential, both to empower others and to maintain the credibility of the change effort as a whole.

Error 6: Not Systematically Planning for, and Creating, Short-Term Wins

Real transformation takes time, and a renewal effort risks losing momentum if there are no short-term goals to meet and celebrate. Most people won't go on the long march unless they see compelling evidence within 12 to 24 months that the journey is producing expected results. Without short-term wins, too many people give up or actively join the ranks of those people who have been resisting change.

One to two years into a successful transformation effort, you find quality beginning to go up on certain indices or the decline in net income stopping. You find some successful new product introductions or an upward shift in market share. You find an impressive productivity improvement or a statistically higher customer-satisfaction rating. But whatever the case, the win is unambiguous. The result is not just a judgment call that can be discounted by those opposing change.

Creating short-term wins is different from hoping for short-term wins. The latter is passive, the former active. In a successful transformation, managers actively look for ways to obtain clear performance improvements, establish goals in the yearly planning system, achieve the objectives, and reward the people involved with recognition, promotions, and even money. For example, the guiding coalition at a U.S. manufacturing company produced a highly visible and successful new product introduction about 20 months after the start of its renewal effort. The new product was selected about six months into the effort because it met multiple criteria: it could be designed and launched in a relatively short period; it could be handled by a small team of people who were devoted to the new vision; it had upside potential; and the new product-development team could operate outside the established departmental structure without practical problems. Little was left to chance, and the win boosted the credibility of the renewal process.

Managers often complain about being forced to produce short-term wins, but I've found that pressure can be a useful element in a change effort. When it becomes clear to people that major change will take a long time, urgency levels can drop. Commitments to produce short-term wins help keep the urgency level up and force detailed analytical thinking that can clarify or revise visions.

Error 7: Declaring Victory Too Soon

After a few years of hard work, managers may be tempted to declare victory with the first clear performance improvement. While celebrating a win is fine, declaring the war won can be catastrophic. Until changes sink deeply into a company's culture, a process that can take five to 10 years, new approaches are fragile and subject to regression.

In the recent past, I have watched a dozen change efforts operate under the reengineering theme. In all but two cases, victory was declared and the expensive consultants were paid and thanked when the first major project was completed after two to three years. Within two more years, the useful changes that had been introduced slowly disappeared. In two of the 10 cases, it's hard to find any trace of the reengineering work today.

Over the past 20 years, I've seen the same sort of thing happen to huge quality projects, organizational development efforts, and more. Typically, the problems start early in the process: the urgency level is not intense enough, the guiding coalition is not powerful enough, and the vision is not clear enough. But it is the premature victory celebration that kills momentum. And then the powerful forces associated with tradition take over.

Ironically, it is often a combination of change initiators and change resisters that creates the premature victory celebration. In their enthusiasm over a clear sign of progress, the initiators go overboard. They are then joined by resisters, who are quick to spot any opportunity to stop change. After the celebration is over, the resisters point to the victory as a sign that the war has been won and the troops should be sent home. Weary troops allow themselves to be convinced that they won. Once home, the foot soldiers are reluctant to climb back on the ships. Soon thereafter, change comes to a halt, and tradition creeps back in.

Instead of declaring victory, leaders of successful efforts use the credibility afforded by short-term wins to tackle even bigger problems. They go after systems and structures that are not consistent with the transformation vision and have not been confronted before. They pay great attention to who is promoted, who is hired, and how people are developed. They include new reengineering projects that are even bigger in scope than the initial ones. They understand that renewal efforts take not months but years. In fact, in one of the most successful transformations that I have ever seen, we quantified the amount of change that occurred each year over a seven-year period. On a scale of 1 (low) to 10 (high), year one received a 2, year two a 4, year three a 3, year four a 7, year five an 8, year six a 4, and year seven a 2. The peak came in year five, fully 36 months after the first set of visible wins.

Error 8: Not Anchoring Changes in the Corporation's Culture

In the final analysis, change sticks when it becomes "the way we do things around here," when it seeps into the bloodstream of the corporate body. Until new behaviors are rooted in social norms and shared values, they are subject to degradation as soon as the pressure for change is removed.

Two factors are particularly important in institutionalizing change in corporate culture. The first is a conscious attempt to show people how the new approaches, behaviors, and attitudes have helped improve performance. When people are left on their own to make the connections, they sometimes create very inaccurate links. For example, because results improved while charismatic Harry was boss, the troops link his mostly idiosyncratic style with those results instead of seeing how their own improved customer service and productivity were instrumental. Helping people see the right connections requires communication. Indeed, one company was relentless, and it paid off enormously. Time was spent at every major management meeting to discuss why performance was increasing. The company newspaper ran article after article showing how changes had boosted earnings.

The second factor is taking sufficient time to make sure that the next generation of top management really does personify the new approach. If the requirements for promotion don't change, renewal rarely lasts. One bad succession decision at the top of an organization can undermine a decade of hard work. Poor succession decisions are possible when boards of directors are not an integral part of the renewal effort. In at least three instances I have seen, the champion for change was the retiring executive, and although his successor was not a resister, he was not a change champion. Because the boards did not understand the transformations in any detail, they could not see that their choices were not good fits. The retiring executive in one case tried unsuccessfully to talk his board into a less seasoned candidate who better personified the transformation. In the other two cases, the CEOs did not resist the boards' choices, because they felt the transformation could not be undone by their successors. They were wrong. Within two years, signs of renewal began to disappear at both companies.

. . .

There are still more mistakes that people make, but these eight are the big ones. I realize that in a short article everything is made to sound a bit too simplistic. In reality, even successful change efforts are messy and full of surprises. But just as a relatively simple vision is needed to guide people through a major change, so a vision of the change process can reduce the error rate. And fewer errors can spell the difference between success and failure.

Originally published in May–June 1995. Reprint R0701J

2

Transformations That Work

by Michael Mankins and Patrick Litre

Nearly every major corporation has embarked on some sort of transformation in recent years. By our estimates, at any given time more than a third of large organizations have a transformation program underway. When asked, roughly 50% of CEOs we've interviewed report that their company has undertaken two or more major change efforts within the past five years, with nearly 20% reporting three or more.

Unfortunately, most transformation programs aren't all that transformative. Though they typically start with great fanfare—complete with big announcements and proclamations of wholesale change—most fail to deliver. Our research indicates that only 12% of major change programs produce lasting results. Too often, leadership accepts disappointing outcomes and moves on, only to launch another program in a few years' time. One prominent U.S. bank, for example, has initiated three substantial restructuring programs in the span of just four years, yet all of them have fallen flat.

It doesn't have to be this way. Over the past two decades we've worked with dozens of companies that have effectively transformed their businesses and studied hundreds of others that have attempted to. Our analysis has revealed six important differences between the programs that worked and those that didn't. In this article we'll explain why so many ambitious change initiatives come up short and outline the steps that leading companies are taking to defy the odds and realize the full promise of transformation.

Underwhelming Results

In late 2023, Bain & Company completed the second of two comprehensive surveys of 300 large companies worldwide that had attempted transformations. The first survey had taken place a decade earlier. The participating companies included both Bain clients and nonclients. The findings highlighted two concerning trends.

> *Less failure, but not more success.* In the 1990s John Kotter and other scholars identified the most common reasons for ineffective transformation attempts—notably, a lack of urgency, insufficient leadership, limited vision, poor communication, and a shortage of "quick wins." Many companies have taken steps to avoid those pitfalls, often seeking outside advisory support. As a result, companies are experiencing fewer outright failures in their transformation endeavors. If we define "failure" as achieving less than half of what leadership aimed for, then only 13% of

Idea in Brief

The Problem
Although companies frequently engage in transformation initiatives, few are actually transformative. Research indicates that only 12% of major change programs produce lasting results.

Why It Happens
Leaders are increasingly content with incremental improvements. As a result, they experience fewer outright failures but equally fewer real transformations.

The Solution
To deliver, change programs must treat transformation as a continuous process, build it into the company's operating rhythm, explicitly manage organizational energy, state aspirations rather than set targets, drive change from the middle out, and be funded by serious capital investments.

recent transformation programs can be labeled as such. That's a significant improvement from the 38% rate observed in 2013 and can be attributed to lessons learned over the years.

But there's a catch. Despite the decline in outright failures, success rates have not risen. If "success" is defined as meeting or exceeding leadership's expectations, then only one in eight transformations can be considered successful—and that rate has remained constant since 2013.

An acceptance of mediocrity. The percentage of transformation programs with so-so outcomes—that is, those that achieved more than 50% but less than 100% of their targets—increased from 50% in 2013 to 75% in 2023. Instead of pushing their organizations to deliver more, many senior leaders seem to settle for improved but still unexceptional performance. While that reaction is understandable, it often signals to employees that if they wait long enough, the status quo will be restored. Worse, it breeds cynicism that undermines the success of future change efforts.

Six Critical Practices

Clearly, the prevailing approach to transformation in most companies is not yielding the desired results. It's time for a new model—one incorporating six practices that our research has shown are key to successful programs.

1. Treating transformation as a continuous process

Most transformation efforts are structured as discrete programs—with a clear beginning and end. Top management sets an ambitious goal, defines a series of initiatives designed to meet it, assigns leaders to manage the change, and then monitors performance until the program is complete. It's an approach inspired by the work of the psychologist Kurt Lewin, who believed that the process of change entails (1) creating the perception that a change is needed, (2) moving toward the new desired behavior, and (3) solidifying that new behavior as the norm. This became widely known as the "unfreeze-change-refreeze" model.

Although that model may have made sense when most business transformations were transitory—that is, a temporary deviation from "normal"—or if the change involved managing the implementation of, say, a new enterprise resource planning system, it's not well suited to deliver major change in today's highly dynamic environment. Most companies are (or should be) in a state of constant transformation. It's simply no longer possible to refreeze and step aside. The most successful efforts recognize

Transformation efforts are still missing the mark

In 2013 and 2023, Bain & Company conducted surveys of the transformation initiatives of 300 large companies worldwide. The companies included both Bain clients and nonclients. The results reveal that despite everything companies have learned from research on what derails change programs, very few transformation efforts achieve their goals.

	Met or exceeded expectations	Settled for mediocre results	Failed to deliver
2013	12%	50	38
2023	12%	75	13

that transformation must be continuous and orchestrate their programs accordingly.

Dell Technologies is a case in point. When Michael Dell took the company private, in 2013, he knew he wanted to transform the PC maker into a broad-based leader in infrastructure technology. He also recognized that to do so he needed his team to keep stretching to drive the next level of performance.

Starting in 2014, Dell's executive leadership meetings centered on what was referred to as the Dell Agenda. This agenda amounted to a backlog of the most critical issues the company was confronting at the time and, by implication, the most important changes Dell had to make to transform successfully. Some issues, such as the need to simplify Dell's product portfolio and transition from a made-to-order to a made-to-stock approach, pertained to day-to-day operations. Others, like defining a new go-to-market structure for the company's direct sales force, were organizational in nature. Finally, many, such as determining how to strengthen the company's position in the rapidly growing, high-margin storage segment, involved strategic opportunities.

What made the Dell Agenda particularly noteworthy was its evergreen nature. When an issue was successfully resolved, it was removed, and a new issue took its place. This ongoing process of addressing operational, organizational, and strategic issues produced extraordinary results. From 2014 to 2023, Dell Technologies experienced a dramatic increase in market value, achieving more than 10-fold growth. The surge in value was a testament to the company's newly established leadership positions in areas such as commercial PCs, servers, storage solutions, and other critical infrastructure technologies.

2. Building transformation into the company's operating rhythm

Too often transformations are viewed as separate from company operations and handled by a distinct program-management office. In most instances, however, working on both should be considered part of every manager's day job.

Consider the approach Alan Mulally took to successfully lead the transformation of Ford Motor Company from 2006 to 2014. Shortly after taking the helm, he introduced a rigorous business plan review (BPR) process, which involved weekly meetings with the entire senior leadership team. The BPR played a pivotal role in aligning the team around a compelling vision and a comprehensive strategy known as One Ford.

The BPR ingrained the implementation of One Ford into the company's operating rhythm. As Mulally noted, "Everyone knew the plan, the status against that plan, and all the areas that needed special attention. Everyone was working together to change the reds to yellows and greens."

Under One Ford the company divested itself of Aston Martin, Jaguar, Land Rover, and Volvo. It terminated its passenger-vehicle joint venture with Mazda and discontinued the Mercury brand. Ford also streamlined its vehicle platforms and standardized components across its models, which resulted in significant cost savings and improved product quality. The proceeds from asset sales and the savings from restructuring, along with external financing, were channeled into creating a "balanced business" of cars, trucks, and SUVs. The company revitalized its iconic brands, including the Ford F-150 pickup and the Mustang, transforming itself from a near-bankrupt relic into an industry leader.

During Mulally's tenure, Ford rebounded from a $12.7 billion loss to a $6.3 billion pretax profit. Though its stock price fell during the global financial crisis, it shot up 800% from its low point, and when Mulally left it was nearly double what it had been when he started.

3. Explicitly managing organizational energy

Transformations fizzle when they consume more energy than they generate. That's why their tendency to continually disrupt the work routines of the same group of individuals is problematic. Over time that group may start to ignore further requests for change or even actively resist them. Our research shows that if an organization tries to change more than two primary routines simultaneously, the odds of failure increase dramatically. For example, consider a scenario in which a company's sales force is asked to sell in newly defined territories while also promoting an expanded portfolio of products and services. In such a situation it's highly likely that sales productivity will drop. Still, despite its importance, organizational energy is rarely managed effectively during transformations.

In successful programs leaders explicitly identify the employees and functions that will be most impacted by each aspect of the initiative and ensure that no group is expected to alter multiple routines at once. Changes are carefully sequenced to limit disruption and prevent widespread organizational fatigue. Success is recognized and rewarded along the way to build energy and enthusiasm for the effort.

Take the transformation of Virgin Australia. In April 2020, just a few months into the Covid-19 pandemic, the company entered voluntary administration as a bankrupt carrier. That September, Virgin was acquired by the U.S. private equity firm Bain Capital (an entity entirely separate from our firm), and by the end of November, Jayne Hrdlicka had been appointed CEO. Under her leadership the company reorganized itself as a much leaner, midmarket carrier. Once it had turned the corner it expanded its fleet by 60%, hired thousands of new employees, opened many new routes, and completely reimagined its customers' experience. Such massive changes could have caused debilitating disruptions had leadership not been meticulous about managing organizational energy.

At the start of the process, every aspect of Virgin Australia's overhaul was carefully sequenced. The airline made significant investments in new planes and technology, restructured its head office, revamped its marketing and sales function, bolstered its procurement team's capabilities, and introduced new customer-service innovations. Virgin's leadership assessed how each change would affect employees and consciously scheduled the hundreds of initiatives involved to avoid overburdening any one part of the organization at any one time. Unnecessary or lower-priority efforts were put on hold, either temporarily or permanently, freeing up organizational bandwidth. Leadership applied a simple rule of thumb: Prioritize the changes that were most crucial to passengers and de-emphasize or eliminate those that weren't. The strategic staging and focus allowed Virgin Australia to move quickly without exhausting its people.

Hrdlicka and her team also actively engaged the organization throughout the transformation, tapping into Virgin Australia's unique "Virgin Flair" culture. They encouraged employees to contribute new ideas for making Virgin "the most-loved airline in Australia." Great ideas were celebrated, and the inclusive approach injected passion and energy into the team's work, significantly accelerating the pace of change. Frontline staff and executives shared in the success of the transformation, receiving bonuses and other financial rewards in recognition of their contributions to the turnaround.

4. Using aspirations, not just targets, to stretch management's thinking

In typical transformation efforts, especially turnarounds and restructurings, the initial step involves examining external benchmarks. These are then used to set top-down targets for cost and head-count reductions, and the organization is tasked with figuring out how to meet them. While that approach may appear rigorous and data-driven, it seldom sparks transformative thinking. Relying on benchmarks tends to confine "the art of the possible" to what others have already achieved, effectively setting the bar too low.

True transformation calls for breakthrough thinking and pushing beyond current practices, often with the help of new technology. Consider Adobe, the $18 billion developer of software for creative services professionals. In 2011, when it declared its intent to shift its entire product line to the cloud, the strategy was deemed unusually ambitious, if not revolutionary. There were few benchmarks that Adobe could refer to—only the aspiration of fundamentally reshaping the company's business model.

Shantanu Narayen, Adobe's CEO, challenged his management team to reinvent the company. Historically, Adobe's formula of selling software like Photoshop to creative professionals at attractive prices had been highly successful. However, Narayen recognized that clinging to the past would not be a winning business strategy. Drawing on his extensive knowledge of the industry and the company, he set the goal of transitioning 100% of Adobe's products to a web-based subscription model. The company would be among the first to adopt the software-as-a-service (SaaS) approach.

This bold ambition unified and motivated everyone at Adobe. Every facet of the business had to grapple with the question, How do we need to do this differently? Transitioning to the cloud significantly affected the company's product development, operations, and go-to-market strategies. For instance, Adobe had traditionally introduced new features whenever a new software version was released, typically every 18 to 24 months. But in the cloud, products could be continuously updated, tested, and released, necessitating a more agile and scrum-based approach to product development.

In addition, Adobe had to invest in cloud-based components that would facilitate seamless downloads of products because customers still needed to have many applications on their desktops. And the way that Adobe engaged with its customers had to change. Its value proposition was reorganized around delivering high-quality service, not merely introducing new features. Aspects of it like uptime, availability, disaster recovery, and security all became pivotal. Much closer collaboration among the functional groups contributing to the overall customer experience, including product management, engineering, marketing, and IT—which all had previously operated separately—was also required.

Adobe continues to transform itself, lately by harnessing breakthroughs in generative AI. In 2023 alone the company introduced 100 new features and updates for its software, including many advanced AI-powered tools. It has expanded Firefly, its AI product line, with three new image generators. Beyond the "wow factor," the wide range and high quality of these innovations have firmly established Adobe as the leading maker of creative tools for professionals.

The results have been truly impressive. Since Narayen became the CEO, Adobe's market value has shot to more than $250 billion from just $24 billion—and the company's average annual total shareholder return (TSR) has been more than 15%. This compares very favorably with the tech-heavy Nasdaq's TSR of just under 9% in the same period. What's more, Adobe's transformation has reshaped the entire software landscape. Nowadays nearly every software company, ranging from Autodesk to Microsoft, has followed Adobe's pioneering lead.

5. Driving change from the middle out

Most transformation programs are top-down: Upper management sets targets and relies on lower organizational levels to figure out how to meet them. Initiatives are then typically executed from the bottom up. While this approach can yield effective ways to cut waste, it rarely produces lasting results. Why? Because enduring improvement requires changes in both the work being done and how it is accomplished. Cross-company intelligence and deep experience are needed to identify those changes, and that calls for a "middle-out" approach.

Senior executives frequently are too far removed from day-to-day operations to understand what truly needs to change. Consequently, top-down solutions tend to be superficial or at least short-lived. Frontline managers, meanwhile, often lack the contextual understanding to challenge existing processes, and so trim around the edges rather than propose major changes. But midlevel executives tend to have enough experience to see the shortcomings in current operations—and aren't so close to the ground that they get lost in the weeds.

Good practices lead to better outcomes

Across Bain & Company's 2023 sample of transformations, efforts that incorporated at least three of six key practices reported higher rates of success than efforts that incorporated two or fewer. The success rate of efforts that incorporated at least five practices was even higher.

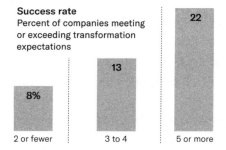

Success rate
Percent of companies meeting or exceeding transformation expectations

2 or fewer	3 to 4	5 or more
8%	13	22

Number of practices (listed below) reflected in transformation effort

Treating transformation as a continuous process	Building it into the company's operating rhythm	Explicitly managing organizational energy
Using aspirations, not just targets, to set expectations	Driving change from the middle out	Accessing substantial external capital from the start

Amgen, the $27 billion global biopharma company, is a case in point. In 2013 its CEO, Bob Bradway, and his team set out to reshape the company, which was more than 30 years old and grappling with the expiration of the patents on several of its most successful drugs. The goal was to reposition Amgen as an agile, patient-centered powerhouse capable of developing groundbreaking drugs quickly.

For each transformation initiative, Bradway and his team selected two midlevel leaders—a VP-level "initiative lead" and a director-level "initiative liaison." These leaders were to make the transformation effort their primary focus. Their selection was rigorous: A "draft," coordinated by the chief transformation officer and the chief human resources officer, was conducted by the CEO and all his direct reports. Eligible executives had to be among the highest rated at Amgen, with proven ability to tackle the most-pressing challenges.

Once the initiative leads and liaisons were in place, teams with the necessary capabilities and expertise were assembled. Leadership emphasized the importance of assigning the best talent to each transformation initiative. This ensured that the teams had the skills to drive meaningful change quickly. Soon the transformation process became a vehicle for testing and developing the next generation of leadership within the company. Many of the initiative leads and liaisons have since moved into senior roles at Amgen.

The middle-out approach surfaced better solutions at Amgen. The team overhauling the company's critical process-development capability offers a great example. Its breakthroughs included such fundamental changes as the consolidation of 17 functions into seven, the closure of five sites, the integration of 25 disparate systems into one new platform, and the implementation of three new cycle-time-reduction processes across the company. Its efforts were a significant departure from previous transformation initiatives at Amgen, which had typically led to modest changes to established practices and processes.

The results have been impressive. From 2013 to 2022 the company doubled the number of approved medicines in its portfolio—from 13 to 27. Many more of its drugs are blockbusters. In 2013, Amgen had only three drugs that generated $1 billion or more in sales. By 2022 it had nine. Significantly, the transformation is still ongoing, with Bradway and his team constantly pushing Amgen to greater heights, as evidenced by its $28 billion acquisition of Horizon Therapeutics.

6. Accessing substantial external capital from the start

Transforming a business is often expensive. Mulally borrowed $24 billion to fund Ford's transformation in 2006, and Michael Dell invested more than $60 billion to turn Dell into a leader in infrastructure technology in 2017.

In our study nearly all failed transformations were underfunded. Many leaders tried to finance them through cost-cutting measures. While that strategy may sound appealing, it typically falls short. Efficiency gains and waste reduction alone usually can't provide enough financial resources.

In contrast, nearly all successful transformations tapped the capital markets. External capital played a crucial role in fueling T-Mobile's growth from 2013 to 2020, for instance. Shortly after John Legere took the reins as CEO in 2012, he and his team acknowledged that a substantial investment was required to pull off the turnaround the company needed. At the time, T-Mobile lagged far behind Verizon and AT&T, with only a third of the wireless subscribers of either carrier. One major problem was that T-Mobile had not supported the iPhone when it became ubiquitous. "Before I joined T-Mobile it was the fastest-shrinking wireless company in America," Legere told *Investor's Business Daily*.

Avoiding the common mistake of relying solely on internal cost-cutting measures, Legere and his team decided to borrow $7 billion to initiate a comprehensive transformation. They set out to redefine T-Mobile as the "uncarrier" by eliminating hated industry practices that benefited carriers but harmed consumers. The company started including taxes and fees in its price quotes to eliminate surprises for customers. Unlimited service became standard, and contracts and global roaming charges were abolished. The iPhone was integrated into the T-Mobile network, and the company invested heavily in acquiring spectrum to enhance coverage. Finally, T-Mobile secured an additional $19 billion to fund its $66 billion acquisition of its U.S. telecom rival Sprint in 2020.

Though the transformation required significant investment, the returns were extraordinary. From 2013 to 2019 (Legere's last full year as CEO), the company's earnings soared 1,000%. Subscriber numbers more than doubled, from 33 million to 86 million. That growth far outpaced that of AT&T and Verizon over the same period. The share price of T-Mobile also rose by more than 400% during Legere's tenure, significantly outperforming the S&P 500's 150% gain. During that time T-Mobile's performance even surpassed Apple's.

. . .

Transformation programs often promise breakthrough results, but most never realize them. The successful ones adopt an approach that fundamentally differs from the approach at other companies. Their leaders view change as a continuous process, integrating it into the company's operating rhythm. They understand that organizational energy is a scarce resource and manage it diligently, and they keep the focus on driving the transformation from the middle out. Never forgetting that major change requires major investments, they secure external capital early (and often). In short, successful transformations employ a transformative strategy—a must for companies aiming for enduring success in today's ever-changing world.

Originally published in May–June 2024. Reprint R2403E

QUICK READ

Let Go of What Made Your Company Great

by Vijay Govindarajan

How can an organization both exploit *and* explore? Managers, consultants, and academics around the world have long wrestled with this question. Some have responded by developing a concept known as "ambidexterity," an organizational capability of fulfilling both managerial imperatives at once. But simultaneously managing today's business while creating tomorrow's goes beyond being ambidextrous. There is a third, even more intractable problem: letting go of what made you great.

Managers exploiting current businesses develop mindsets based on what they have experienced in the past. Such mindsets become further embedded in systems, structures, processes, and cultures that are self-perpetuating. It's hard for managers, especially those who excel in the current system, to explore new uncharted terrain. And even harder for them to notice that many entrenched mindsets have lost relevance in changing circumstances that require exploring for new businesses. Bottom line: *Before you can create, you must forget.*

Based on my work with dozens of *Fortune* 500 companies and other organizations, I have found that "unlearning," although indispensable, is extremely difficult. When the Willow Creek Association saw its once-popular nondenominational conferences and training decline in attendance and revenues, the organization made the difficult and painful but necessary decision to eliminate two-thirds of its 150-person workforce in order to rid itself of obsolete knowledge and prepare the organization for new sources of growth. A similarly difficult, but necessary, "letting go" challenge: GE's decision to divest its once-successful financial service businesses.

Letting go requires tough actions like the ones in my examples to bring the organizational reflex circuitry out of autopilot. These decisions are among the hardest ones that executives have to make, but there are some proven ways to approach an organization's forgetting challenge. The appropriate solution to employ depends on the magnitude of the challenge and how much of the organization is affected by the challenge.

A Big Challenge for the Entire Organization

The entire organization has to forget a lot of what made it successful in the past. This is the most formidable forgetting challenge. For instance, in the early 1990s, the Mahindra Group faced a forgetting problem of nearly gargantuan dimensions: the end of the so-called "License Raj" system. Under License Raj, the Indian government licensed and tightly regulated domestic businesses while excluding foreign competitors. The License Raj was intended to allow Indian businesses to emerge and flourish under protected conditions, but it had the unintended effect of inducing inefficiency and complacency. As the system ended,

Idea in Brief

The Problem
Many companies struggle to balance maintaining their current success and innovating for the future.

The Solution
Leaders must recognize when to let go of practices and strategies that once made the company great but are now hindering progress. By fostering a culture of adaptability and experimentation, they can implement new approaches that better align with emerging market demands and technological advancements.

The Payoff
Companies that successfully navigate this transition can become more resilient and better positioned to capitalize on new opportunities.

---

the most urgent imperative for CEO Anand Mahindra was to shake the entire company out of its complacency.

To address a big forgetting challenge such as this, here are two techniques that work.

Do something major to catch your company's attention

A company's past is often deeply rooted in its culture, comprising habitual processes, rituals, and belief systems. That's why forgetting the past can require shocking the culture out of its torpor. Mahindra settled on a change that was bound to be difficult and controversial—an explosive mix of symbolism, cherished tradition, and employee entitlement: the annual Diwali bonus. These bonuses are extra compensation given to workers on the occasion of major Hindu festivals; they are entitlements not correlated with performance. When Mahindra stopped handing out the Diwali bonus, it had the impact of shooting a rocket through the company. "That was a major turning point," Mahindra said in an interview I did with him for my book *The Three Box Solution*. "That is how we were able to make the entire organization begin to forget the past."

Create win-win incentives

Incentives are a powerful lever to convince people they need to forget the old ways. As United Rentals, the largest equipment rentals company, shifted its strategy to focus more on national customer accounts, it faced a huge forgetting challenge; branch managers needed to forget the fiefdom mentality. CEO Mike Kneeland changed the incentive system for branch managers. Instead of rewarding them for branch performance, their compensation would be based on regional performance. This encouraged a coordinated approach to serving national accounts. (Kneeland established a zero-tolerance policy for any failure to cooperate.)

A Big Challenge for Only Part of the Organization

In this challenge, only part of the organization has to forget a lot. IBM is a good example. By the 1990s, IBM had become the go-to provider of enterprise information technology—hardware, software, and systems integration—for large and midsized businesses. While these core businesses continued to generate cash flow, IBM struggled to find the Next Big Thing. The company could not eradicate the skills and processes that continued to power its core performance engine, but at the same time, it had to enable embryonic growth ideas to forget the orthodoxies of the core.

To solve this forgetting challenge, leaders can create a dedicated team and give them a fresh start. Ideas for nonlinear businesses should not be weighed down by core business rules or expectations. IBM's Emerging Business Opportunities (EBO) process provides cover for experimental business units targeting embryonic markets. The EBO program set up startup-friendly structures as well as a separate set of practices in the areas of organization, leadership/management, resource allocation, strategy development, and performance measurement and motivation. The goal of EBO is not to affect the structures and processes that continue to be useful for the performance engine, but to create protective structures and alternative competencies that allow nonlinear innovations to flourish.

A Smaller Challenge for the Entire Organization

This forgetting challenge is small, but it applies to the entire organization. The customers of United Rentals historically were concentrated in the construction industry—always vulnerable in a downturn. After the Great Recession, the company's strategy shifted to protect it against cyclicality. The construction sector continued to be important, but the entire organization had to forget its 100% dependency on this one industry.

A technique for this forgetting challenge is to practice portfolio reconfiguration. To protect against dips in the construction industry during economic downturns, United Rentals made targeted acquisitions to break into the specialty rentals business (consisting of unusual but essential items, such as heavy-duty pumps used by energy companies and safety equipment used to reinforce newly dug trenches), which were more recession-proof.

A Smaller Challenge for Only Part of the Organization

Relatively speaking, this forgetting challenge presents the least difficulty for companies. Managers can act locally to change the behaviors, systems, or processes that are no longer as relevant to where the company is going in the future. However, leaders should monitor this situation—if only to ensure that this doesn't grow into a larger problem.

. . .

By understanding your company's forgetting challenge in this way—how big is the challenge and how much of the organization is involved—you can develop targeted solutions like the ones I've described. Above all, don't ignore this challenge as you try to innovate your way to a new model. You must have the courage to see the many ways in which the dominant logic of your legacy business can undermine your future business—and help your organization let go of what made it great.

Adapted from hbr.org, April 13, 2016. Reprint H02T7W

Persuade Your Company to Change Before It's Too Late

by Pontus M. A. Siren, Scott D. Anthony, and Utsav Bhatt

There's a paradox facing leaders seeking to transform their organizations as they see their markets begin to change. On one hand, they need convincing data to make the case that transformation is necessary—to show that their companies are about to find themselves on "burning platforms." On the other hand, by the time public data about disruptive trends and market shifts is convincing, the window of opportunity has shrunk, if not disappeared. And when companies actually are on burning platforms, their leaders confront a harsh reality: Burning platforms inhibit change by increasing rigidity at the very moment when flexibility is crucial. The lesson: Avoid ever ending up on a burning platform. But that requires leaders to act before compelling data is widely available.

Berkeley Cox, Michelle Mahoney, and the rest of the leadership team at the Australian arm of King & Wood Mallesons (KWM), a global law firm, faced this exact problem several years ago. They were starting to pick up signals that their law practice needed to change dramatically, but convincing data was still scarce. The three of us worked with KWM Australia to generate and interpret what we call "private data," or unique insights that clarified the change brewing beneath the industry's surface. This article describes the approach we took and details specific methods other leaders can use to similarly motivate their organizations to address shifts before the evidence of them is abundantly clear.

The Nature of the Challenge

Business leaders face a problem that's familiar to investors and political leaders: In periods of uncertainty the availability of information and the freedom to act are inversely correlated—or, in simpler terms, as data increases, your ability to act decreases.

Let's say your company is deciding whether to commit a large amount of its resources to entering a new market such as driverless cars. As competitors' moves and degree of success provide information about the market (its size, profitability, and growth rate), they simultaneously constrict your freedom to seize opportunities in it; with each move your rivals are building difficult-to-replicate capabilities and establishing strong positions in the most attractive market segments.

We have created a simple conceptual model to help companies map out where they stand when it comes to their knowledge and their ability to act. We call it the *information-action paradox*. A thought experiment contrasting Entrepreneurial Ellen and Corporatized Chris illustrates how it works. Entrepreneurial

Idea in Brief

The Challenge
Many organizations resist change until it's too late, often due to complacency, fear of the unknown, or lack of sufficient evidence to convince decision-makers to act. This reluctance can lead to missed opportunities and declining competitiveness.

The Solution
Leaders must recognize the signs of stagnation and act decisively to drive transformation before external pressures force their hand. They can build a compelling case for change by clearly communicating the risks of inaction, highlighting the benefits of change, and creating a sense of urgency. Engaging stakeholders at all levels and fostering a culture that values adaptability and innovation are also crucial.

The Payoff
Organizations that embrace change proactively are better positioned to capitalize on new opportunities and mitigate risks.

Ellen has a low threshold of proof, meaning she is willing to act with a low amount of data. Why? Well, she's an entrepreneur! She doesn't have to convince a wide range of stakeholders of the need to act. She's also starting with a blank sheet of paper, so she doesn't worry about the effect her actions will have on her established operations. She can take bold, intuitive risks. Corporatized Chris has a higher threshold of proof, for three reasons. First, he has basic human biases such as status quo bias (the inclination to keep things the way they are) and loss aversion (the tendency to care more about avoiding losses than about receiving equivalent gains). While Ellen innately has those biases too, she hasn't yet established her business, so she doesn't have much to lose, and she is hoping to create a status quo worth preserving. Second, Chris has to deal with multiple stakeholders

> **The information-action paradox**
>
> The more data that's widely available in a market, the lower the freedom to act on it becomes, because others see the same opportunities and risks and respond to them. The information threshold is not the same at every company. An entrepreneur like Ellen, who doesn't have much business to lose or many stakeholders she has to get buy-in from, can act with less information. But an executive of a more risk-averse established company, like Chris, needs more information to persuade himself and his stakeholders that bold moves are necessary.
>
>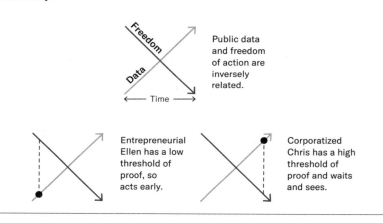

who reinforce his biases. And finally, his organization makes decisions using traditional financial tools, which further bias organizations against investing in innovation, according to Clayton Christensen, the late Harvard Business School professor who cofounded our firm, Innosight. (See "Innovation Killers: How Financial Tools Destroy Your Capacity to Do New Things," HBR, January 2008.)

It's possible, of course, that Ellen is wrong, in which case Chris can say, "I told you so." However, if she is right, by the time the data crosses Chris's threshold of proof, his company will be on the proverbial burning platform. And by then, Ellen and other entrepreneurial leaders will have carved up the most attractive market spaces, built technology advantages that are expensive to copy, hired the best talent, and so on.

The Situation at KWM

Back in 2018, Cox was in his second year as the elected leader of about 150 partners and 750 lawyers at KWM Australia, a partnership that serves corporate clients, including many blue-chip organizations, in that country. Mahoney, a 20-year veteran of KWM with deep technological expertise, was in her third year as KWM Australia's executive director of innovation.

Four signs suggested that significant change was coming to the market. First, the number of companies promising to use technologies such as machine learning to deliver routine legal services more effectively and efficiently (known as "legal tech") was on the rise. Second, many clients, tired of high bills, had built internal capabilities to handle significant chunks of legal work. The increased sophistication of in-house counsels made them more open to alternative solutions that would deliver better value. Third, leading accounting firms such as KPMG and PwC, attracted by the margins earned by law firms, had publicly announced their intent to build up their own legal services practices. Fourth, young lawyers were expressing more and more frustration with long hours of often mind-numbing work such as proofreading documents and cross-checking citations, prompting firms to try to address the historically backbreaking nature of the associate job.

Cox was certain that those dynamics posed a material threat to the firm's fundamental operations. But his personal conviction wasn't enough to get the firm to take bold steps to counter that danger. That's because the kind of core transformation

KWM needed wasn't about making a daring leap into a new market, like Amazon's entry into cloud computing. Nor was it about reshuffling a portfolio of offerings, as Intuit did when it bought Mint.com and sold its personal-financial software package, Quicken. Such major moves can be driven by an individual's vision or a small team of decision-makers. But KWM Australia could change its way of operating only if all its partners and lawyers started thinking and acting differently, and they had no obvious pressure to do so. KWM was firmly positioned as a top-tier firm in Australia, had a strong balance sheet, and was considered an employer of choice by Australian law school graduates. In short, its business was strong, and other public indicators such as industry associations' market growth forecasts suggested it would stay healthy.

Cox knew he had his work cut out for him. "Lawyers are risk-averse by nature," he notes. "That's why they're good at what they do. They also look for perfect information to make decisions, but in this environment, as in many environments, information is not perfect." If Cox waited until perfect data validated his intuition to change course, it would be too late to change course.

This quandary isn't unique to legal services. Think about a university president pushing for distributed digital education. "What about student outcomes?" faculty members will say. Once edutech providers demonstrate conclusively that distributed digital education provides equal or superior learning outcomes, opportunities for universities will narrow. Or consider the head of a chain of automobile service stations who thinks the business should pivot to caring for electric vehicles. Though it seems like a pretty good bet that the number of electric vehicles on the road will someday surpass the number of vehicles with internal combustion engines, exactly when is uncertain. And if the head of the chain waits until that moment arrives, other entrants are very likely to have already seized the opportunity.

Building Collective Conviction at KWM

So how can leaders get their companies to act before their businesses are on bona fide burning platforms? By generating private data (as KWM did) and lowering the threshold of proof.

Generating private data

As we've noted, public data, the kind found in industry reports, rarely produces the will to act early. But private data can be a game changer.

There are three broad categories of private data. The first is *qualitative data*. This includes testimonials from customers who provide insight about their future actions and behind-the-scenes stories of purchasing decisions that were "near misses"—meaning customers almost made a different choice. It also includes research that hasn't yet been published in scientific journals and proprietary intelligence on the progress of start-ups that are still operating in "stealth" mode. Yet another useful source of private data is recently hired employees, who often are more closely connected to market-shifting trends.

The second category is *quantitative data*, such as analyses of purchasing behavior in specific customer segments or analyses that track shifting market sentiment by identifying patterns in comments on chat boards or employee review sites like Glassdoor.

The final category is *proprietary models* that process and analyze data in unique ways. For example, a financial model that predicts the future impact of not taking action to deal with trends today can surface the hidden risk in continuing to follow the current strategy.

KWM Australia's extensive analysis of its proprietary client data showed that the firm's overall growth masked its commercial challenges at the low end of the market, where disruptive change often begins. The firm also developed client case studies using detailed "voice of the client" interviews, which further illustrated changing industry dynamics. They revealed, for instance, that the gap between the quality of KWM's work and the work of emerging competitors was perceived to be narrowing rapidly.

When such private data is shared at the right time in the right way (more on that in a bit), it can help make industry disruption feel much more front and center than it appears in the public data and thus can strengthen the collective resolve about the need for change.

Lowering the threshold of proof

Even the best private data is unlikely to produce a level of certainty close to that generated by a detailed financial model whose inputs are all demonstrated facts.

There are two ways to lower the threshold of proof enough to motivate an organization to take early action. The first is to use frameworks and models to make sense of incomplete information. The information-action paradox framework served this purpose at KWM Australia. In the first half of 2018 we shared it at two major partner meetings and asked the partners to discuss the question "How far to the right are we on the chart?" It was a simple way to make people more aware of why it was so hard to make decisions during uncertainty. It also helped the group realize the degree to which a significant number of colleagues *already* felt that change was crucial. For example, in one meeting almost 20% of the 110 attendees said that the firm was now on the right side of the model, where there was more than enough data to suggest it was imperative to act. The people pushing for change, it turned out, had access to their own private data from conversations with current and prospective clients. That information, however, was locked in their individual heads. Once they shared it with everyone else, momentum for change began to build.

Another framework that helped KWM interpret faint signals was Christensen's disruptive innovation model, which shows that disruptive change often starts in less-demanding market segments or among customers that have historically lacked the skills or wealth to consume existing solutions (people Christensen called "nonconsumers"). After explaining this model to groups of the firm's leaders, we outlined specific indicators that an industry is in the early stages of major upheaval. Then we shared the insights generated from the firm's private data and asked each group to discuss the degree to which they amounted to early warning signs. The disruptive innovation model helped people spot trends that might otherwise be dismissed as the usual gradual churn of the market. And with each meeting, the collective conviction that there was indeed a clear need to change grew.

A second way to lower the threshold involves techniques that help groups align around a course of action in the face of uncertainty. At KWM Australia, we drew on tips described in the November–December 2018 HBR article "Unite Your Senior Team" (which one of us, Anthony, coauthored). A key enabler was developing a common language around select strategic issues. The firm's partners had robust discussions about what various terms, such as "legal tech," meant. This is critical because when a team doesn't take the time to precisely define language, people often simply talk past one another.

It's also crucial to ensure that there's space to surface and debate key areas of misalignment. One memorable example of this came during a February 2018 meeting of the board of KWM Australia. After hearing about key disruptive trends, board members were asked to give their view on how much of the profit pool should be invested in innovation. They shared their individual estimates using a mobile-phone-based polling app. Answers ranged from roughly 1% to 10%. We then asked the directors who gave the highest and lowest numbers to explain the assumptions underpinning their responses. The discussion helped highlight divergent viewpoints on topics like the degree to which partners closer to retirement would be willing to invest in the future and the pace of disruptive change. ("We've been talking about change for 20 years," one board member said. "Why will it be different this time?") That helped the board determine what private data would be most critical for subsequent discussions.

Signals in private data can often be dismissed as market noise. That's why it's important to look at it in structured discussions. At KWM Australia these helped the partners agree on where the industry was, the pace of change, and what that meant for where the industry would be in the future. A summary question—"Does anyone think that the legal industry won't change significantly in the next five to 10 years?"—helped cement the conviction to act while there was still time.

The Impact at KWM

It took KWM Australia about a year to get everyone on the same page. (Leadership didn't expect or demand an overnight shift.) While Cox and his team, with input from our firm, created a draft perspective about the future direction of the law firm, they also created space for discussion, debate, and disagreement, allowing collective ownership of the need to change to spread through informed dialogue. Eventually the partners came to the consensus that to navigate market disruption and deliver better outcomes for clients, the firm had to become tech-enabled and infuse cutting-edge artificial intelligence and smart-contracting tools into its day-to-day practices. With Cox, Mahoney, and Mark McNamara, a senior partner who headed the private equity practice, playing key leadership roles, KWM launched a three-pronged effort to advance its transformation.

First, it introduced targeted behavioral interventions to encourage the adoption of productivity tools. They included a program called "Use It or Lose It," which allowed lawyers to get credit against their billable-hour targets for up to 30 hours of training, experimentation, or coaching on legal tech.

Second, the firm created programs to support its transformation. One of them tackled the way the billable-hour model can implicitly penalize efficiency and make using technology appear to be against a lawyer's best interests. To address that, KWM introduced a "multiplier" model, which increases the weighting of tech-enabled hours worked by lawyers. A lawyer who does 10 hours of work using artificial intelligence to review a contract might get credited with 15 hours of traditional work (without any additional cost to the client). That program was coupled with broader moves toward fixed-fee engagements that further encouraged the use of technology.

Third, KWM Australia implemented a comprehensive communication program. For example, in November 2019 Cox and McNamara laid out the logic behind the case for change in a

3,700-word document that was organized into eight sections followed by two appendixes. The firm also engaged a communications change specialist (a novel approach for a law firm) to simplify key messages and communicate them clearly and consistently across the organization. And it asked newly elected partners to evaluate warning signs of disruptive change and describe the future business model of their practices.

By September 2021, KWM Australia had made significant progress in its effort to transform itself. Nearly 300 fresh graduates and young lawyers (about 30% of the staff) had gone through its "digital-literacy boot camp." The firm had invited many of them to act as "reverse mentors" for more-seasoned lawyers. It had removed billable-hour targets for newly hired lawyers, a clear sign to the market that it intended to thoroughly transform an operating model that had been successful for more than a century.

By that time the multiplier model had gained traction and had been used by teams of lawyers serving close to 500 clients. The firm had also built a centralized transformation hub that housed more than 130 videos exploring various aspects of legal technology and providing case studies and had dubbed more than 100 lawyers who had demonstrated proficiency in digital transformation and emerging legal technologies "digital legal eagles." A high-profile award ceremony had shone a spotlight on teams that had pushed the technological frontier and transformed the client experience. And earlier in the year, in recognition of its digital-first approach to client service and people management, KWM had been named the most innovative law firm in Asia-Pacific by the *Financial Times*.

Remember, all this took place inside a law firm that faced no obvious reason to change given its strong performance, happy clients, and sterling reputation as an employer of choice in the industry.

. . .

A recent cross-industry survey of more than 300 global leaders conducted by Innosight found that 72% felt that they needed to transform their core offering or business model. The most pressing obstacle to success cited by this group was allocating enough resources to change efforts—an indication that their leadership teams lacked the conviction to take action. As the KWM Australia story demonstrates, generating private data and lowering the threshold of proof can help leaders build such conviction before the need for change becomes glaringly apparent. This approach can accelerate strategic transformation and save businesses from ending up on burning platforms.

Originally published in January–February 2022. Reprint S22013

4

Getting Reorgs Right

by Stephen Heidari-Robinson and Suzanne Heywood

Chances are you've experienced at least one and possibly several company reorganizations. Reorgs can be a great way to unlock value: Two-thirds of them deliver at least some performance improvement, and with change in the business environment accelerating, they are becoming more and more common. As John Ferraro, the former COO of Ernst & Young, told us, "Every company today is being disrupted and so must frequently reorganize to keep up with the incredible pace of change. Those that can do this well will thrive in the current environment and be tomorrow's winners."

At the same time, few reorgs are entirely successful. According to a McKinsey survey we conducted, more than 80% fail to deliver the hoped-for value in the time planned, and 10% cause real damage to the company. More important, they can be damned miserable experiences for employees. Research suggests that reorgs—and the uncertainty they provoke about the future—can cause greater stress and anxiety than layoffs, leading in about 60% of cases to noticeably reduced productivity. In our experience, this occurs because the leaders of reorgs don't specify their objectives clearly enough, miss some of the key actions (for example, forgetting processes and people in their focus on reporting lines), or do things in the wrong order (such as choosing the way forward before assessing the strengths and weaknesses of what they already have). Yet the pitfalls they succumb to are common and entirely predictable.

During our careers we have seen many reorgs, read lots of books and articles about which type of organization companies should adopt, and watched countless fads come and go. But we've found precious little advice on how to actually run a reorg. Many practitioners assert that reorgs are so fluid and dynamic that it would be naive and counterproductive to try to impose a process on them. Our conclusion, based on experience and analysis, is the opposite: *How* you go about your reorg is as important as—and sometimes more important than—*what* you do.

To help maximize the value and minimize the misery of reorgs, we have developed a simple five-step process for running them. We don't claim that this is rocket science; indeed, we're proud to assert that it is not. But we do know that companies need to take a more systematic approach if reorgs are to deliver on their potential. And we have personally advised companies through the five steps in more than 25 reorganizations—companies with 100,000 employees or a handful, in the Americas, Europe, the Middle East, Asia, and Africa. In fact, survey data shows that companies using this process are three times as likely as others to achieve their desired results.

Idea in Brief

The Problem

Most reorganizations fail to deliver on their initial promise, for several reasons: They run into employee resistance, they're not given sufficient resources, and they distract people from day-to-day work.

What's Missing

The biggest reason for disappointing results, though, is that few organizations follow a rigorous, disciplined process—even though reorgs are a common occurrence in large companies.

The Solution

The authors propose a five-step process: Begin with a profit and loss estimate, inventory your strengths and weaknesses, consider multiple options for the new organization, focus special attention on execution, and assume you'll need to make course corrections.

Step 1: Develop a Profit and Loss Statement

A reorganization is not some esoteric pursuit but a business initiative like any other—similar to a marketing push, a product launch, or a capital project. So you should start by defining the benefits, the costs, and the time to deliver. Remember that the costs are not just those of employees and consultants involved in the reorg; they also include the human cost of change and the disruption it can create in your business. We have accumulated data on these factors for 1,800 reorgs. Previous reorgs in your company, and the experience of employees who have worked elsewhere, can help you estimate the impact.

It may seem like common sense to weigh costs and benefits, but according to McKinsey research, only 15% of executives set detailed business targets for their reorgs, and 17% of reorgs are launched at the whim of an executive or because the leadership team believes the company needs to be shaken up—reasons that typically lead to problems. Both the objective of the reorg and the process for running it should be as fair, transparent, and reasonable as possible. Not only is that right for your employees, but it will make them much more likely to accept, get behind, and improve your ideas.

Let's consider the case of an international media company. Its reorg started with an exercise to define the revenue-improvement opportunity worldwide. At the time, it was a federation of local businesses with no net growth. Teams of company strategists and business experts estimated that a more integrated global approach could significantly grow flat revenue and set a specific target for the reorg. The cost of internal project support and external consultants was agreed on, and a timeline was proposed: The new organization would ideally be set up and running within a year—in time to deliver results in the latter half of a new three-year business plan. A reorg P&L had been constructed.

Step 2: Understand Current Weaknesses and Strengths

No surgeon would start operating on a patient before conducting tests and reaching a diagnosis. And when excising a tumor, they would be careful to avoid removing healthy tissue. So should it be with a reorg. Unfortunately, this step is often skipped, which means that changes at best have no impact and at worst undermine previous strengths. Those companies that do take the time to self-diagnose before embarking on major surgery typically rely on interviews with senior executives to get input. That's a good place to start, but we would recommend adding an electronic

> ## Why Reorgs Fail
>
> A McKinsey survey of 1,800 executives identified the most common pitfalls for reorganizations (in order of frequency).
>
> 1. Employees actively resist the changes.
> 2. Insufficient resources—people, time, money—are devoted to the effort.
> 3. Employees are distracted from their day-to-day activities, and individual productivity declines.
> 4. Leaders actively resist the changes.
> 5. The org chart changes, but the way people work stays the same.
> 6. Employees leave because of the reorg.
> 7. Unplanned activities, such as an unforeseen need to change IT systems or to communicate the changes in multiple languages, disrupt implementation.

survey, which will enable you to capture a companywide range of input and to see the differences between headquarters and the front line and between levels and geographies. In addition, since reorgs are all about performance improvement, take time to understand how outcomes vary across the business. For example, if you have multiple sales teams, which one is most successful and why? These inputs will help you decide what to retain, what to roll out elsewhere, and what to change.

The media company interviewed 23 leaders across all parts of the business, using a "card sort" in which 40 attributes of the existing organization—such as innovation, local responsiveness, and leadership bench strength—were written on cards, and interviewees were asked to categorize them as "significant issue," "somewhat of an issue," or "not an issue." This process highlighted problems that the company was having finding the right people to fill roles, sharing information across geographies, and incentivizing innovation. Yet the company scored well on P&L accountability and local responsiveness—strengths that needed to be preserved. (Although these interviews were helpful, we realized in retrospect that the responses represented too thin a slice of the organization. In subsequent reorgs elsewhere in the company, we used electronic survey tools that captured a much wider range of opinions across levels, business units, and geographies.)

Step 3: Consider Multiple Options

The next step is to decide on the design of your new organization. You can take one of two approaches. You can change the entire organizational model—for example, organizing by customer segments instead of along geographical lines. That approach is best if your organization is completely broken (although such cases are rare) or is facing a fundamental market shift that cannot be navigated under the current model. Or you can change only those elements that don't work—for example, altering the executive board process for financial approvals, removing a layer of middle management, or upgrading your frontline leaders while leaving the rest of the organization unchanged. That approach is best when the overall organization works well or the focus is on cutting costs. The analysis you conducted in the first two steps will help you make the choice. If in doubt, choose the second approach.

A common mistake in this step is to focus on *what the organization looks like* (its reporting structure, for instance) and forget about *how it works* (management and business processes and

Communicating the Reorg

To be considerate of your employees and get their buy-in, the process needs to be fair and transparent.

- *Plan communications across all steps of the reorg.* Start with transparent information: what will happen, when, and whom it will affect. Try to excite people only after it's clear what they will be doing (in step 4). If you try earlier, they won't listen, and you'll come across as detached.

- *Focus your communications on topics that matter to your people, not just to you.* Sadly, few of your employees will care as much as you do about return on investment capital. You have to find something about the change that motivates them. Elon Musk says of the companies he's founded and their organization going forward, "People at Tesla, SolarCity, and SpaceX feel that they are doing things that matter: If we can advance sustainable energy by 10 years, that is 10 years of less carbon."

- *Make sure communication is in person, not just in email cascades.* Too often your carefully crafted emails will get no further than your direct reports' inboxes. Make sure your leaders are spelling out the practicalities of the reorg for their staffs and answering employees' questions.

- *Communication should be two-way.* This is especially true in steps 4 and 5, when you are trying to get the details of the reorg right and ensure that it is working properly. On-the-ground feedback from your staff is essential. Reflecting on his experience of reorganizations, John Browne, the former CEO of BP, told us, "Your people are sometimes aware of what is going on before you are, so you need to listen to them."

systems; and the numbers, capabilities, mindsets, and behaviors of its people). In our experience, the latter is usually more important than the former.

Finally, you should explicitly choose from a number of options for exactly how to restructure your organization. Any solution has its downsides; only by weighing alternatives will you see what you might gain and what you might lose. Too often leaders realize late in the day that they missed something in the original design. If they insist on adding it later, the company may end up with a push-me-pull-you design that blunts the effectiveness of the new organization and unnecessarily complicates people's lives.

At the media company, the top 12 global business leaders gathered offsite to debate the relative merits of three options. They were assigned to teams—one for each option—and asked to advocate for their given option (no negatives allowed) and to answer questions from the other teams. Leaders who were expected to dislike a particular model were deliberately put on the team for that model: For example, the most autonomous local leaders were put on the team for the most centralized option.

During the debate it became increasingly clear that the most centralized model was the only one that would provide sufficient benefits to justify the disruption and the human cost of the change. At the end of the meeting, nine of the 12 leaders voted for that option, and the specific concerns of the remaining three were accounted for in the detailed design. After the exercise, the CEO reflected, "There is always more than one right answer, so how you bring people along and get them behind the new organization is really important. Through the workshop, we came to a good answer, and—perhaps more important—we brought our leadership team along with us."

Step 4: Get the Plumbing and Wiring Right

After step 3, most executives stand back, trusting their teams to handle the details of the new organization and the transition plan. External consultants usually clock off at this point as well. Yet we've repeatedly found—and a 2014 McKinsey survey confirmed—that step 4 is the hardest part of the reorg to get right. The secret is knowing all the elements that need to change and planning the changes in the right sequence. For example, you must create new job descriptions before the jobs can be filled, and they must be filled before you start location moves, potentially across countries. Similarly, you need to agree on how your P&L will be managed before you can allocate costs and revenues, and only then can you design the required IT changes, test them, and ultimately implement them. All this takes effort, and if you miss something in any area of the detailed design—structural changes, processes and systems, or people—you may either hold up the whole reorg or find that your new organization has been launched half born. In many cases the organization has changed but the systems (notably the P&L) have not, and leaders are left driving a fast car with no steering wheel.

Executives at the media company put in extra effort at this stage. The CEO continued to spend significant time on the reorganization; leaders were appointed to their new roles before the switchover so that they could begin to own and steer the work; and the reorg project team members moved from managing the process out of HQ to visiting the regional businesses that would be most difficult to transition and working with the local management teams to hammer out the plan. In particular, they took pains to understand how the P&L of each local business broke down and who would be responsible for each revenue or cost lever in the new organization. Of course, this process highlighted previously unappreciated challenges—such as the fact that customer segmentation, which was clear at the global level, was sometimes less clear in a few countries where customer groups blended together; and the need to account for acquisitions that were midway through integration when the detailed design was developed. This prompted the company to make some tweaks and exceptions to its new structure and processes and to lengthen transition periods for some units. But its leaders stood fast on something we've found to be a fundamental rule for successful reorgs: 80% of the business (by revenue, profit, and people) must make the change, and the exceptions must not be allowed to hold up progress for the rest.

Step 5: Launch, Learn, and Course Correct

No matter how much thought and preparation you put into a reorg, it's unrealistic to expect that it will work perfectly from the beginning. As Nancy McKinstry, the CEO of another client—the information services company Wolters Kluwer—says, "You have to live with and digest it, and rapidly course correct when you find issues." That doesn't mean you need to do a 180 in the design as soon as you hit a snag. But you do need to encourage everyone to spot and point out the new organization's teething problems, openly debate solutions, and implement the appropriate fixes as soon as possible, in line with the logic of your original plans.

The media company's reorg was altered in several ways after the launch. One activity around developing content, which had been allocated to a new business line, was returned to its original unit, because synergies that had been persuasive on paper turned out to be less impressive in practice. Back-office activities, untouched by the revenue-focused reorg, were further consolidated afterward, bringing cost savings into the mix.

Within three years of the reorg, the company had met its goal: The issue of flat revenue had been addressed and the growth target met.

Conclusion

If you're contemplating a reorg, you owe it to your shareholders and employees to follow a rigorous process rather than winging it, as so many leaders do. You'll make better decisions, keep your people more involved and engaged, and capture more value.

Originally published in November 2016. Reprint R1611F

QUICK READ

Six Steps for Gaining Employee Buy-In

by Andrea Belk Olson

Most advice about building internal support for organizational change reiterates perfunctory platitudes, reminding leaders to communicate reasons for the change, or even to be excited about the change themselves. But in working with hundreds of companies going through organization change, I've learned that this approach is simply not enough. In fact, research shows that this narrow approach often results in a wave of employee cynicism, doubt, distrust, and negativity, which can relegate change efforts to a slow and painful death.

What too many leaders fail to realize is that, while a certain level of skepticism to change is natural, heading it off from the start is the only way to counter it. But how?

The most successful organizations I've worked with have done it by creating a culture of change acceptance long before they intend to introduce any changes. They do this by addressing six components of culture: legitimacy, ownership, relevance, attainability, authenticity, and impartiality. Here's how it works.

Legitimacy: Engage Your Organizational Change Influencers

When introducing change, organizations typically rely on their leadership teams, overlooking those individuals who may not hold a leadership title but are key influencers of company culture.

Whether they are middle managers, key sales personnel, or even the office receptionist, these people can make or break your plan. Why? Because unlike those in traditional leadership roles, these informal influencers wield more power to shape organizational change acceptance, often through intelligence, networking abilities, or simply the respect they hold within company ranks.

Folding in those influencers early in the change process will not only build confidence across the organization via trusted yet informal leaders but also establish a foundation for change rooted in reliable voices.

Ownership: Provide Everyone a Table Stake

An open mic at a town hall meeting after you've decided what will be done does not amount to input. What's more, your employees likely know that you're not taking their suggestions seriously. Holding these meetings likely hurts your change initiative.

Research, however, shows that when people have actual agency in shaping a change, they are significantly more likely to embrace it. Instead of unidirectional town halls, hold a series of small interactive discussions where departments can determine potential roadblocks and define how the change can come to life for their area of responsibility. This provides them a way to tailor and adapt execution to fit their own unique circumstances, conditions, and restraints.

Idea in Brief

The Challenge
Organizational change is often met with resistance from employees, and simply communicating the reasons for the change usually isn't sufficient to overcome it.

The Solution
Leaders must create a culture of change acceptance before implementing any new initiative. To do this, executives should engage employees early and often to address their concerns, get their feedback and ideas, involve them in decision-making, provide relevant training and resources, and articulate the initiative's benefits for them.

The Payoff
Organizations that successfully gain employee buy-in are more likely to see their change initiatives succeed—which leads to improved morale, increased productivity, and a stronger alignment between the organization's objectives and its workforce.

Relevance: Focus on Latent Change

Organizations have two types of change: one they are championing today, and others on the perpetual back burner, too unwieldy, complex, or politicized to tackle. While it feels counterintuitive, incorporating this second group can be the easiest way to increase buy-in for the first.

If a current change effort can be tied to other changes that have been festering and never addressed, you're in for a win. By coupling components of known needs to today's change, you reframe the change as crucial and integral, rather than just extra work added to the pile. Further, it reinforces that leadership recognizes chronic frontline challenges and doesn't simply brush them under the rug.

Attainability: Create a Series of Micro-Changes

The flip side of this advice is to make sure your change is attainable. Often, change can be viewed as insurmountable due to its perceived magnitude. For instance, an IT department may have a deeply complex and intertwined technological infrastructure, limiting its ability to see the change as anything but intrusive, upending, or even catastrophic.

A useful approach, in many cases, is to break change efforts into a series of micro-changes. Any segmentation approach that enables change to be more digestible, achievable, and manageable will help reduce resistance by making progress attainable in the short term, while establishing a sense of accomplishment for the long term.

Authenticity: Embody Behaviors That Support the Change

Logos, posters, stickers, T-shirts, and other swag—it's all fodder for supposedly building buy-in and excitement. But people know what it signals and are prepared to lie in wait until the initial excitement passes and things return to the status quo.

Instead of glossing over change with superficial gifts, represent what the change embodies through action. For example, if a change focuses on "giving more back to our community," translate it into direct behaviors, from paid volunteer hours to employee donation matching. Providing behavioral illustrations of what the change represents transforms it from something stated to something acted upon.

Impartiality: Establish a Neutral Change Facilitator

Finally, be prepared for conflict. When the CEO or C-suite leadership solely have the oversight of change, individual concerns and questions get funneled to direct supervisors. Then, as conflicts between departments arise, teams jockey to have their opinion or perspective blessed over another, whether it's beneficial to the larger change or not.

Bringing in a third party can help neutralize internal office politics, posturing, and infighting. Serving as part moderator, part engagement manager, and part counselor, they are there to keep decisions unbiased and eliminate favoritism. This third party can be a trusted consultant or veteran industry expert, but ideally someone from outside the organization.

What Happens When Employees Buy In to Change

Although change is never easy, how leaders approach it makes a significant difference to whether it's embraced or rejected. By addressing the organizational buy-in context, it's much easier to move past resistance and stagnation, because your path forward will be shaped by realities rather than banalities. Having employees buy in to change doesn't simply make implementation easier but rather forges an immutable and reciprocal relationship that pays infinite dividends. Without this, future endeavors will require reengaging, perpetuating the cycle of resistance. Remember, trust takes months to build and only seconds to break.

Adapted from "Getting Employee Buy-In for Organizational Change" on hbr.org, February 6, 2023. Reprint H07H2K

5

Storytelling That Drives Bold Change

by Frances X. Frei and Anne Morriss

Let's say you're a leader with an urgent organizational problem—anything from a broken culture to a product that no longer fits your market. You've taken several steps toward a solution: You've identified the core issue and surfaced roadblocks to progress. You've run smart experiments that point the way forward. You've tapped the knowledge and earned the trust of everyone whose help you'll need, including people whose thinking is different from yours. With all that accomplished, you're ready to tackle a critical challenge: crafting a story so clear and compelling that it will harness your organization's energy and direct it toward change.

Research has shown that storytelling has a remarkable ability to connect people and inspire them to take action. "Our species thinks in metaphors and learns through stories," the anthropologist Mary Catherine Bateson has written. Tim O'Brien, who has won acclaim for his books about the Vietnam War, put it this way: "Storytelling is the essential human activity. The harder the situation, the more essential it is." When your organization needs to make a big change, stories will help you convey not only why it needs to transform but also what the future will look like in specific, vivid terms.

In this article we outline an effective way to leverage the power of storytelling, drawing on decades of combined experience helping senior executives lead large-scale change initiatives. There are four key steps: Understand your story so well that you can describe it in simple terms; honor the past; articulate a mandate for change; and lay out a rigorous and optimistic path forward. Let's explore each of them in turn.

Understand Deeply, Describe Simply

This, we've observed in our work advising leaders, is the foundation of persuasive communication. If you understand something but can describe it only in complex or jargony language, you'll reach just the subset of people with expertise in the topic.

Consider T-Mobile's transformation from a company teetering on the edge of irrelevance to the serious player it is today. After he was named CEO, in 2012, John Legere began listening in daily on customer service calls. As was widely reported in the press at the time, the experience led him to a fundamental truth about the wireless industry: People hated it. They resented being trapped in confusing contracts and hit with hidden fees. So he decided to offer clear service plans and transparent charges, among other innovations—in short, to become everything the industry wasn't. Legere understood the story of T-Mobile's change at such a profound level that he could communicate it in a single word: *uncarrier*.

Idea in Brief

The Challenge
Before you can solve an urgent organizational problem, you need to take a crucial step: craft a clear, compelling story that harnesses everyone's energy and directs it toward change.

How to Meet It
First, understand your story so deeply that you can describe it simply. Then honor your organization's past, articulate a mandate for change, and describe a rigorous and optimistic way forward.

The Payoff
Depending on the measurement used, up to 70% of organizational change efforts fail. These steps will greatly increase your chances of defying the odds.

When you think about the change you want to lead, ask yourself this: Can I capture my vision in a page? A paragraph? A word? The French philosopher Blaise Pascal once apologized for writing a long letter, explaining that he hadn't had time to write a short one. Your first task is to craft the equivalent of a short letter—even though it may take you extra time.

Honor Your Past

Your next step toward creating the future is to revisit the past, counterintuitive though that may seem. The process has two distinct stages.

Acknowledge the good parts of your history

It's easy to become so focused on the things you want to change that you forget to communicate what you *don't* want to. To get everyone on board with your ideas, you need to show that you truly understand the organization, starting with the good stuff.

There will always be self-appointed gatekeepers who are resistant to change—typically, valuable employees who have long institutional memories, care deeply about the organization, and worry about what might get lost in the transition. To bring them along, make it clear that you intend to preserve what's best about the company. Even the most logical change initiative can be unsettling and disruptive to those who'll be affected. Show people that you get it. We suggest having at least one gatekeeper stay close to you throughout the process so that you witness that person's concerns firsthand, which will make you more likely to respect and account for them.

In a study of large organizational change initiatives, the University of Amsterdam's Merlijn Venus and colleagues found that employees commonly feared their soon-to-be-transformed company would no longer be the organization they valued and identified with. The greater the uncertainty around the initiative, the greater the anxiety. Leaders were most effective in building support for change when they also emphasized continuity, the researchers found.

When Dara Khosrowshahi hosted his first town hall meeting as Uber's new CEO, in 2017, it might have been tempting to highlight the firm's missteps and position himself as its savior. Instead he promised to "retain the edge that made Uber a force of nature," a remark met with thunderous applause. (Disclosure: One of us, Frances, is a former Uber employee.)

We were struck by Khosrowshahi's grace in that meeting. Follow his lead and show some sensitivity toward the people who aren't so sure about your plans for change: the skeptics, the resisters, and the simply scared. Honor the past they're holding on to, and they may gradually loosen their grip.

Reckon with the not-so-good parts

If your firm has lost the trust of any stakeholders, you'll need to rebuild it and earn the right to push forward. Spurred on by a courageous blog post by the software engineer Susan Fowler, in which she detailed her experience of harassment at Uber, Khosrowshahi combined his commitment to retain what was best about the company with a pledge to lead cultural change.

If your initiative is to capture employees' hearts and minds, you'll need to confront your organization's history with both optimism and honesty. Optimism means revealing your belief in a better tomorrow. Honesty means taking full responsibility for the things that went wrong and acknowledging the human costs of those mistakes.

For an example of taking clear, unequivocal responsibility for a painful past, we often point to the video game developer Riot Games (a company we've advised). In 2018 the organization issued a plainspoken apology on its website in response to public allegations of a fractured and sexist culture. "To all those we've let down . . . we're sorry," it began. "We're sorry that Riot hasn't always been—or wasn't—the place we promised you. And we're sorry it took so long for us to hear you."

Riot stands in stark contrast to many other companies that are called out for missteps. For instance, when the data engineer and whistleblower Frances Haugen publicly challenged Facebook (now Meta) to work harder to protect its most vulnerable users, the company's first response was to try to undermine her credibility. A tide of public frustration, a drop in the firm's stock price, and an increase in regulatory scrutiny followed. A good-faith attempt to engage with Haugen's rigorously documented charges would probably have yielded better results.

You don't need to have all the answers to begin addressing the difficult parts of your company's past. You do need to be willing to look at them unflinchingly and deal honorably with whatever you find. When Riot included with its apology a pledge to make the company "a place we can all be proud of," it didn't have all the details of its plan worked out. But it was definite about the fact that it needed one.

Provide a Clear and Compelling Mandate for Change

Now that you've honored the past—the good, the bad, and the ugly—and opened your stakeholders' minds at least somewhat to your message, it's time to share your rationale for creating a different future.

Begin by reflecting on the "why" of your plan. What problem are you trying to solve? What's the cost of not solving it? Your answers must be persuasive enough to override the comfort of familiar beliefs and behaviors. Among the challenges you may encounter is one put forward by Harvard Business School's Rosabeth Moss Kanter in Kanter's Law: *Everything looks like a failure in the middle.* You need to give people solid reasons to press on.

In 2010, faced with slumping sales and an anemic stock price, the new CEO of Domino's, Patrick Doyle, knew that to mount a successful turnaround he'd need to break through the malaise permeating the company culture. The chain was delivering handsomely on its promise to get customers pizza in record time. But as one reporter noted, "You then had to eat it." People had decided the pizza tasted so bad that in consumer tests, they rated the same pies lower when they knew they were from Domino's rather than a competing brand.

The conventional move would have been to quietly chip away at the problem while downplaying consumers' negative reactions. But Doyle and his team realized that a shock to the system was in order, so they decided to shine a bright light on customers' frustrations. They shared some of the scathing feedback in national ads and on a digital billboard in New York's Times Square. Comments like "worst excuse for pizza I've ever had" and "tastes like cardboard" scrolled in massive letters across its screen.

That bold move fueled fast, transformative change by making the need for it vividly clear. Stakeholders could not escape the fact that Domino's had a problem. Russell Weiner, the CMO at the time (he's now CEO), told *Inc.* magazine, "By saying what we said about the pizza, we blew up the bridge. That's what made it so much more powerful. If it didn't work out, there was no place to retreat to. There was no going back."

By leveling with consumers instead of trying to spin the situation, the company demonstrated its authenticity and engaged its market directly. Customers were given an essential truth-telling role in the campaign—and an excellent reason to pay attention to what happened next. After all, they'd been enlisted to co-create the needed fix—dubbed "Pizza Turnaround," which hit the right deeply/simply notes.

What happened next was good for everyone. The chain's pizzas got a whole lot better, Pizza Turnaround grew same-store sales by more than 10% within a year, and the company's stock price took off.

Describe a Rigorous and Optimistic Way Forward

Your next step is to get into the weeds of your plan. What persuaded you to choose the road ahead? How confident are you that it's passable? In addressing those questions, you want to convey two things: rigor and, again, optimism. Data can help you demonstrate the first to stakeholders. Get comfortable with the numbers and pick just a few to use as plot points in your story. When it comes to data in storytelling, less is more.

When the Danish firm Ørsted set out to transform itself from an old-school power company into a leading provider of renewable energy, its management focused on a single ratio: 85%. The firm had historically generated that share of its energy from fossil fuels. In 2008 the leaders of the company (then called DONG Energy) decided to work toward flipping that ratio so that 85% would come from sustainable sources such as wind and solar. It labeled the initiative "85/15."

In communicating the plan, the company's leaders addressed hard truths about its strategic exposures, including climate change and the inevitable depletion of fossil fuel stores, with boldness and rigor. Henrik Poulsen, who was the CEO of Ørsted from 2012 to 2020, used that approach to enlist an initially skeptical workforce. "We set a long-term vision, then translate it into a strategic business ambition with tangible targets to guide it," he wrote in an online newspaper ad. "Then we roll that back into action items for each employee to focus on over the next year." Ørsted aimed to reach its goal in 30 years. It did so in a decade.

Now for the optimism part. Jeff Bezos famously asks his team to make the case for new ideas in structured six-page memos. Less famously, he asks people to pair those memos with hypothetical press releases, in part to test for the presence of genuine enthusiasm. In converting stakeholders to your vision, remember: Optimism is an infectious emotion that can be one of your most effective tools.

According to Gallup research, just 15% of U.S. employees "strongly agree" that their organization's leadership makes them enthusiastic about the future. To improve that number in your own organization, rigorously and optimistically describe your way forward.

Put the Pieces of Your Story Together

Now that you've taken those steps, it's time to combine the elements of your vision into a narrative and get others behind it. Ursula Burns, the CEO of Xerox from 2009 to 2016, who led the company through a major pivot from manufacturing to services, knows how effective that can be. Stories were the chief currency of her leadership. "One of the things I learned," she told the 2021 California Conference for Women, "was that stories matter, communications matter. Putting things in context matters." Burns spent countless hours meeting with stakeholders from around the world and making it clear that massive change was the only way forward—and that there was a better Xerox ahead. "Telling people the reality of what's going on and giving them hope by providing them with the vision . . . for what it's going to look like when we get through this is fundamental," she told attendees. "It's foundational to having people follow you."

Like Burns, you can assemble a change story that will inspire people to follow you. Use the structure we've discussed: Understand deeply and describe simply, honor the past, lay out the mandate for change, and provide a rigorous and optimistic vision for the future. Put your thoughts down on paper and, if practical, do it with your team. Share what you come up with to test and improve it. And remember that your customers are resources, too. Ask trusted ones for feedback—or take inspiration from Domino's and invite members of the public to add their voices to your story.

You needn't limit yourself to words (and the occasional number). When Jan Carlzon led the 1980s turnaround of Scandinavian Airlines (SAS), he circulated a small illustrated pamphlet featuring a sad cartoon plane to convey the company's switch to a strategy anchored in delighting business travelers. As Carlzon detailed in his memoir, his fellow executives worried that SAS's cerebral Scandinavian workforce would reject the comic format and dismiss the message. But the pamphlet was widely embraced and helped the firm chart a course through turbulence and change. Carlzon's effort remains one of the most successful turnarounds in business history.

For a more recent example, consider Marguerite Zabar Mariscal, the CEO of the restaurant and retail brand Momofuku. She commissioned a beautifully designed pocket-size guidebook after the company reached a thousand employees—too many for her to continue relying on intimate storytelling. Every new employee gets a copy of it.

Use words, numbers, cartoons, pictures—anything that helps activate your team—to bring your change story to life. Spark joy in the process, and stay open to the unexpected.

Repeat Yourself

Now tell your story wherever the opportunity arises: in speeches, interviews, town hall meetings, team huddles, one-on-ones. Push yourself outside your comfort zone and experiment with different formats. For example, high-quality videos are now easy for anyone with a smartphone to make, and they can be a powerful tool for showing—rather than simply telling—your story of change.

You'll probably need to communicate far more often than you think you should. In our experience, change leaders generally need to double or triple their pace of strategic messaging.

Why? Frequent communication ensures that busy, distracted stakeholders will internalize your story to the point where it reliably informs their actions. A core objective of change leadership is to set others up to succeed in your absence. That's essential to organizational speed because it means you won't become a bottleneck.

Alan Mulally talked incessantly about his "One Ford" turnaround plan when he was CEO of the car company. He started every meeting by reviewing it, and he had it distributed to every employee on a wallet-sized card. Bryce Hoffman, the author of a book on Mulally's time at Ford, wrote, "After six months, those of us who followed the company had gotten sick of hearing about [it]." When in one interview Hoffman asked Mulally if he'd be sharing something new, the CEO was incredulous. "We're still working on this plan," he replied. "Until we achieve these goals, why would we need another one?" That relentlessness paid off. In less than four years Mulally pulled Ford back from the brink of bankruptcy and made it one of the most profitable automakers in the world.

Research by Harvard Business School's Tsedal Neeley and the University of California's Paul Leonardi validates Mulally's approach. After studying leaders in six companies for 250-plus hours and recording every communication, the pair discovered that leaders who were intentionally redundant moved

> ## Ten Underrated Emotions in Change Narratives
>
> In addition to being powerful tools of persuasion, emotions can ground us and make us more authentic. Here are some that leaders tend to undervalue—in both storytelling for change and beyond.
>
> - *Frustration.* The serial entrepreneur Paul English has tapped into this for every one of his breakthrough ideas. For example, he started the metasearch engine Kayak after spending vast amounts of time combing one airline website after another for flights.
> - *Regret.* This typically relates to our interactions with others. We regret a careless comment or not saying something that could have made a difference. Uncomfortable as this emotion is, it often shows us what to do differently next time.
> - *Enthusiasm.* The most effective change storytellers are evangelical about the future and reveal their excitement at every turn. Don't hold yourself back.
> - *Devotion.* We sometimes withhold the full expression of our devotion—our commitment to someone else's success—in the mistaken belief that it will make it harder to hold that person accountable for performance. It won't.
> - *Happiness.* The late Tony Hsieh built his shoe and clothing empire Zappos on a foundation of happy employees, customers,

their projects forward faster and more smoothly than others. "We're so bred to believe that clarity is the key to being a better communicator," Leonardi told HBR. "It's [actually] about making your presence felt. Employees are getting pulled in many directions and reporting to lots of people and getting tons of communications. So how do you keep your issues top of mind? Redundancy is a way to do that."

and suppliers. Let his legacy be that we listen more closely to the story he came to tell us.

- *Discomfort.* We are wired to avoid this feeling—yet so much good happens outside our comfort zone, whether it's learning something new or confronting an unfamiliar problem. As IBM's then-CEO Ginni Rometty told attendees at Fortune's Most Powerful Women Summit, "Growth and comfort don't coexist."

- *Anger.* This is often a mask for more complicated feelings such as disappointment and sadness. When you're experiencing anger, do some emotional digging. What might be living beneath the anger? What can you learn from it? Can you harness it as a motivating force?

- *Joy.* This is one of NBA coach Steve Kerr's four core team values (along with mindfulness, compassion, and competition), which Kerr credits with fueling the Golden State Warriors' success. That often surprises people—until they see the team cheerfully dominate the court.

- *Fellowship.* Life brings all of us to our knees at some point. We need other people to help us get back up, in big and small ways. That's just as true at work as anywhere else.

- *Grace.* This might take the form of kindness, compassion, or generosity of spirit. It might be a decision to have a difficult conversation—or not to. However it shows up, grace demands that we first practice it on ourselves in order to be credible conduits to others.

Dharmesh Shah, a cofounder of HubSpot, has written, "It took me 20+ years as an entrepreneur to start to recognize the power of repetition—and even then, it's still uncomfortable." (Disclosure: HubSpot is a client of the Leadership Consortium, an organization we started.) That sort of discomfort, Shah notes, signals that you're on the right track. "It's *natural* for it to feel *unnatural*," he continued. "Unnatural, but profoundly necessary." One test of whether you're communicating your change story often enough: Are you sick of hearing yourself talk? The answer should be yes.

Identify and Use Your Emotions

We'll close by talking about emotions—an underexplored part of leading change. Evolution has taught us to pay close attention to one another's feelings, particularly those of people with influence over our security and well-being. That unconscious vigilance can be both an asset and a liability for executives. It means that a leader's optimism is highly infectious—but so are emotions such as stress and anxiety.

Wanting to demonstrate the power of gratitude in the workplace, former PepsiCo CEO Indra Nooyi regularly sent thank-you notes to the *parents* of her senior team members, expressing appreciation for sharing their children with the firm. She wrote more than 400 notes a year. Some of Nooyi's colleagues—high-flying executives with résumés filled with accomplishments—told reporters it was the best thing that had ever happened to them.

Nooyi's notes embody what Daniel Goleman, the psychologist who developed the idea of emotional intelligence, would call *primal leadership*. He has described the phenomenon this way: "The leader's mood is quite literally contagious, spreading quickly and inexorably throughout the business. . . . The same holds true in the office, boardroom, or shop floor; group members inevitably 'catch' feelings from one another." When you're a leader, there's no button to turn off the broadcast feature on your feelings.

Many organizations experienced that reality in the early days of Covid-19. Researchers seeking communication lessons from the crisis surveyed some 800 employees. One finding was that the emotional note leaders hit could make or break an individual's commitment to the firm. "Our leader's reassurances . . . that the company has our backs are inspiring," one person said. "I even used [them] . . . on social media to make sure people knew we are still hiring and that this is the sort of company you want to work for when the going gets tough."

Self-awareness is key to playing the instrument of your emotions and preventing them from sabotaging your change story. Accepting your feelings and integrating them into your actions also builds trust by reinforcing authenticity.

. . .

You may be familiar with this oft-cited statistic: Depending on the measurement used, up to 70% of organizational change efforts fail. But if you create a compelling narrative, you'll greatly increase your chances of defying those odds. Your story can transform your organization by shaping attitudes and beliefs, starting with your own. The story you tell yourself sets the stage for the organizational change you're envisioning. And when you share it skillfully with others, your story starts to become their reality.

Originally published in November–December 2023. Reprint R2306C

QUICK READ

Organize Your Transformation Around Purpose and Benefits

by Antonio Nieto-Rodriguez

A dramatic shift is taking place in industries everywhere: We have left behind a century dominated by increasing efficiency and are now living in an always-changing environment. Operating a business in this environment means having a massive proliferation of change projects.

In a survey of 1,284 executives and project management professionals, the majority of senior executive respondents indicated that the number of change projects in their organizations had exploded over the last five years. Some 85% of the respondents had seen an increase in the number of projects, and out of these respondents, 56% had seen a rise of more than 25%. A full 25% of respondents said that the number of projects had increased by more than 50%. This meteoric growth of projects is affecting not only organizations, but also our professional lives and the very nature of work.

Change management can no longer be ignored, relegated, or misunderstood. These fundamental shifts have created huge anxiety in the workplace and a natural dislike for change projects. Yet, nowadays, continuous transformation is at the center of the strategy of any organization, small, midsize, or large. Everyone at all levels—employees, managers, project managers, senior leaders, and CEOs—must understand and adapt to this shift.

Welcome to the Project Economy and a World Driven by Change

While the number of change projects keeps rising, the failure rates continue to be staggering: According to the Standish Group, only 31% of projects are considered successful. The idea that 69% of change projects result in wasted resources and budgets and unrealized benefits is mind-blowing. It requires that we approach change management in a radically different way, not only from a methodological perspective, but also from organizational, cultural, and pure human perspectives.

In fact, most of the current change management methods were developed for a stable world, where change projects were temporary and added to day-to-day operations, which were always the priority.

New concepts and tools to address change are emerging. I introduce two of them in the *HBR Project Management Handbook*: the importance of the purpose behind any change project, and the focus on the benefits.

Purpose: An Easy-to-Apply Tool to Fire Up Engagement

All change and project management methodologies demand that projects have a well-defined business case with often lengthy, technical, and deliverable-focused goals: for example, a new

Idea in Brief

The Challenge
Organizations have a continual need to evolve, but many change initiatives fail due to a lack of clear purpose and perceived benefits for stakeholders, which leads to resistance and disengagement.

The Solution
Leaders should articulate compelling reasons for the change and outline the tangible benefits for all employees. Doing this requires transparent communication, active listening, and involving stakeholders in the planning and implementation stages to foster a sense of ownership and commitment.

The Payoff
When stakeholders understand the "why" behind the change, they are more likely to support and engage with the process, which will improve its chances of success.

---

software rollout, a new platform, an expansion program, a new set of company values, a reorganization, or a digital transformation project. Most change projects use financial goals, such as a 10% return on investment. Yet these goals don't inspire people to commit passionately to the change initiative.

Besides having a business case, a project should be linked to a higher purpose. People have enormous strengths, and the best leaders know that it's possible to tap into those strengths through hearts and minds. When a project that people work on connects to their inner purpose and passions, they can achieve extraordinary things.

According to the EY Beacon Institute, purpose-driven companies are 2.5 times better at driving innovation and transformation than other companies. At the same time, Deloitte says that, on average, purpose-driven companies report 30% higher levels of innovation and 40% higher levels of workforce retention than their competitors. These statistics are borne out in my own experience: Change initiatives with a higher purpose have significantly higher chances of success than those that don't inspire people. Understanding the purpose and its connection to the overall strategy is not just crucial for deciding whether to invest or whether the transformation makes sense strategically; it is also a key driver for engaging team members and the organization as a whole, motivating them to support the change initiative.

Remember that people don't have to be great at something to be passionate about it. Steve Jobs was not the world's greatest engineer, salesperson, designer, or businessman. But he was uniquely good enough at all these things and was driven by his purpose and passion for doing something far greater. Conversely, a lack of purpose or conviction about a change project can quickly spread from one team member to the rest of the team.

A remarkable example of setting a compelling purpose for an organizational transformation comes from Sony's cofounder Akio Morita. At a time when Japan was seen as a cheap-product-copycat country, Morita established that Sony's purpose was to make Japan known for the quality of its products. Japan—not Sony. Sony's purpose was aimed at a higher dimension than its own company—which was bold yet inspiring to its employees.

An easy method of finding a change project's purpose is to continuously ask, "Why are we doing the project?" Usually, you need to ask this question three to four times to get to the core purpose. For example, consider the introduction of a new client relationship management (CRM) software system. Most change managers will say that the project is about implementing a new CRM system, but that's not *why* we do the project. Instead, ask,

"Why do we want the CRM system?" The answer may be, "To manage our data more effectively, providing a single source of truth for our customer information." You've just gone to a higher-level purpose. Next, ask yourself again why you want this outcome, and you may come up with "To provide a more personalized and responsive service." You just went to a higher level again, and a higher priority of thinking based on what's more essential for your company. Then ask again: "Why do we want to provide a more personalized service?" "Because we want our customers to be delighted with our services and retain them over the long term, which will lead to higher revenues."

We've now moved the purpose of our project from installing a new CRM system to a project that will increase customer satisfaction and improve sales performance. What a difference. Now, we have a project whose purpose connects with the organization's strategy and will motivate project team members.

Once you've gotten to the real reason behind your change project, ask, "By when?" and "How much?" Here's an example: "We'll increase customer satisfaction by 50% for our next customer survey, which will take place in five months." Now you have a SMART purpose—a specific, measurable, actionable, relevant, and time-based goal.

Every successful change project needs at least one clearly articulated SMART purpose.

Benefits: The Key to Obtaining Buy-In from Stakeholders

Traditional change management practices have focused on the inputs and outputs—things like plans, schedules, budgets, deliverables, teams, and more. A change initiative is considered successful if it is delivered on time, on budget, and within scope. Yet, what matters most are the outcomes and benefits delivered, such as happier employees, returning customers, more sustainable practices, and so on.

A great example of putting the focus on benefits is sustainability transformation. Sustainability has become one of the most profound challenges of our time and a priority topic on most CEOs' agendas. Consider this example from Procter & Gamble (P&G): Marc Pritchard, a top marketer at P&G, has described how the world's biggest consumer goods company is embracing sustainability to transform its brands. Or, as he puts it, to make P&G "a force for good and a force for growth." As part of its new Ambition 2030 plan, P&G has pledged to make all its packaging fully recyclable or reusable by 2030. The company also plans to use 100% renewable energy and have zero net waste by that time.

While benefits might be easy to claim, they're far more challenging to validate and measure, mainly when they're accruing over time. Since a change project's success should be measured by the benefits achieved, the process you use for identifying and mapping the benefits must be inclusive and transparent.

Each project will bring different benefits to different stakeholders. Change managers and project leaders should identify the main benefit expectations for each key stakeholder early in the transformation. Here is a simple approach to identifying the main benefits of your change projects:

- Develop a benefits card, which is a checklist of the potential benefits of change projects. The figure provides an example of the potential benefits of a digital transformation project.

Organize Your Transformation Around Purpose and Benefits   95

- Instead of defining the expected benefits of your project, meet with your key stakeholders and, with the help of the benefits card, ask them which benefits they would like to obtain from your change project. For instance, in a digital transformation project, the sales manager would like to see an increase in revenues from top customers.

- Ask the key stakeholders to tell you how to measure the benefits and when they would like the benefits delivered. For example, you could have a benefit of enhancing customer experience by increasing the Net Promoter Score from 50 to 80 in five months.

- Show the link between your change initiative, its benefits, and the organization's strategy to help reassure your stakeholders of the project's credibility—for example, how your digital transformation will help your organization increase its competitive advantage.

- Plot the benefits into a benefits plan, which you should use to show progress when communicating with key stakeholders. See the figure for an example.

By using this approach, you'll see that the level of engagement and buy-in for your initiative will significantly increase.

Organizations need to change regardless of whether they are successful or not. They cannot wait years to start obtaining benefits; leaders need to create value faster than ever. Constant transformation has become a top priority. Therefore, change management is now an essential business priority that can't be overlooked or set aside; leaders must start adopting new concepts like purpose and benefits. And they need to urgently develop

Example of the benefits card for a digital transformation project

Each project will bring different benefits to different stakeholders. Change managers and project leaders should use the benefits card to identify the main benefit expectations for each key stakeholder early in the transformation.

Benefit	Objective	Key performance indicators	Example
Improved efficiency	Reduce the time and resources required to complete tasks and processes	• Time-to-complete for key processes • Reduction in manual data entry • Reduction in error rates • Increase in process automation levels • Increase in throughput or productivity	Delta Air Lines implemented a digital transformation project to improve its maintenance processes. It equipped maintenance teams with mobile devices to access real-time information about aircraft maintenance schedules, reducing the time required to complete maintenance tasks and improving operational efficiency. As a result, it saved over $40 million in maintenance costs in the first year.
Increased agility	Improve the organization's ability to respond quickly to changing circumstances	• Time-to-market for new products or services • Number of successful product launches or service offerings • Reduction in time to make business decisions • Increase in speed of adapting to new trends • Number of successful partnerships formed	The clothing retailer Zara used digital transformation to improve its supply chain and reduce the time it took to bring new fashion collections to market. It implemented an end-to-end digital process that allowed the company to quickly analyze customer preferences and trends, design and produce new clothing items, and deliver them to stores in just a few weeks. This allowed Zara to respond rapidly to changes in fashion trends and remain competitive in a fast-paced industry.

Enhanced customer experience	Improve customer satisfaction and loyalty by providing a more personalized and engaging experience	· Customer satisfaction scores · Net Promoter Score (NPS) · Number of repeat customers · Increase in customer engagement levels · Reduction in customer churn rates	The coffee chain Starbucks used digital transformation to enhance the customer experience through its mobile ordering and payment app. The app allows customers to order and pay for their drinks in advance, reducing waiting times and increasing convenience. It also offers personalized recommendations based on previous orders and integrates with the Starbucks Rewards loyalty program, providing customers with incentives to continue using the app.
Increased revenue	Generate more revenue by expanding into new markets, creating new products, or offering new services	· Revenue growth rate · Number of new customers acquired · Sales conversion rates · Average order value (AOV) · Profit margins for new products or services	The financial services company American Express launched a digital transformation initiative to expand its product offerings and improve customer experiences. It developed a suite of digital tools and services, including a mobile app, online banking platform, and digital payment services, to reach new customers and provide more value to existing ones. This resulted in an increase in revenue and a significant improvement in customer satisfaction scores.

Example of a benefits plan for a digital transformation project

Once you have identified the benefits for your key stakeholders, plot them into a benefits plan, which you should use to show progress when communicating with key stakeholders.

○ Intermediate milestones ● Completed milestones

Benefit	Time to completion	Months 1–12
Save $40 million in maintenance costs	7 months	○ $20 million saved (month 4); ● $40 million saved (month 7)
Reduce time-to-market from 12 months to 6 months	4 months	○ Time-to-market: 9 months (month 2); ● Time-to-market: 6 months (month 4)
Increase Net Promoter Score from 50 to 80	5 months	○ NPS 60 (month 3); ○ NPS 70 (month 5); ● NPS 80 (month 5)
Expand product offering to deliver an increase of 30% in revenues from new products	12 months	○ 10% increase (month 4); ○ 20% increase (month 8); ● 30% increase (month 12)
Improve real-time data on client issues to increase product reliability and reduce customer complaints by 80%	6 months	○ 40% reduction (month 4); ● 80% reduction (month 6)
Reduce time spent in meetings by 50% to increase productivity	7 months	○ 20% reduction (month 3); ○ 40% reduction (month 5); ● 50% reduction (month 7)
Increase the number of patents by 25%	12 months	○ 10% increase (month 4); ○ 20% increase (month 8); ● 25% increase (month 12)

change and project management competencies across all levels of an organization, from employees and managers to senior executives. Some visionary leaders have already embarked on this transformation. If you hesitate or wait too long, you might be putting the future of your organization at stake. The one thing that's certain about the future is that change is here to stay.

> Adapted from "Organize Your Change Initiative Around Purpose and Benefits" on hbr.org, May 17, 2023. Reprint H07N6H

6

The Network Secrets of Great Change Agents

by Julie Battilana and Tiziana Casciaro

Change is hard, especially in a large organization. Numerous studies have shown that employees tend instinctively to oppose change initiatives because they disrupt established power structures and ways of getting things done. However, some leaders do succeed—often spectacularly—at transforming their workplaces. What makes them able to exert this sort of influence when the vast majority can't? So many organizations are contemplating turnarounds, restructurings, and strategic shifts these days that it's essential to understand what successful change agents do differently. We set out to gain that insight by focusing on organizations in which size, complexity, and tradition make it exceptionally difficult to achieve reform.

There is perhaps no better example than the UK's National Health Service. Established in 1946, the NHS is an enormous, government-run institution that employs more than a million people in hundreds of units and divisions with deeply rooted, bureaucratic, hierarchical systems. Yet, like other organizations, the NHS has many times attempted to improve the quality, reliability, effectiveness, and value of its services. A recent effort spawned hundreds of initiatives. For each one, a clinical manager—that is, a manager with a background in health care, such as a doctor or a nurse—was responsible for implementation in their workplace.

In tracking 68 of these initiatives for one year after their inception, we discovered some striking predictors of change agents' success. The short story is that their personal networks—their relationships with colleagues—were critical. More specifically, we found that:

1. Change agents who were central in the organization's informal network had a clear advantage, regardless of their position in the formal hierarchy.

2. People who bridged disconnected groups and individuals were more effective at implementing dramatic reforms, while those with cohesive networks were better at instituting minor changes.

3. Being close to "fence-sitters," who were ambivalent about a change, was always beneficial. But close relationships with resisters were a double-edged sword: Such ties helped change agents push through minor initiatives but hindered major change attempts.

We've seen evidence of these phenomena at work in a variety of organizations and industries, from law firms and consultancies to manufacturers and software companies. These three network "secrets" can be useful for any manager, in any position, trying to effect change in their organization.

Idea in Brief

The Question

Large organizations—and the people working in them—tend to resist change. Yet some people are remarkably successful at leading transformation efforts. What makes them so effective?

The Research

An in-depth analysis of change initiatives at the UK's National Health Service revealed that the likelihood of adoption often depended on three characteristics of change agents' networks of informal relationships.

The Findings

Change agents were more successful in the following situations:

- When they were central in the informal network, regardless of their position in the formal hierarchy
- When the nature of their network (either bridging or cohesive) matched the type of change they were pursuing
- When they had close relationships with fence-sitters, or people ambivalent about the change

You Can't Do It Without the Network

Formal authority is, of course, an important source of influence. Previous research has shown how difficult it is for people at the bottom of a typical organization chart—complete with multiple functional groups, hierarchical levels, and prescribed reporting lines—to drive change. But most scholars and practitioners now also recognize the importance of the informal influence that can come from organizational networks. The exhibit below shows both types of relationships among the employees in a unit of a large company. In any group, formal structure and informal networks coexist, each influencing how people get their jobs done. But when it comes to change agents, our study shows that

In the formal hierarchy of one unit in a large company, Lukas holds the most senior position, while Josh is at the bottom of the pyramid. But, as the informal network diagram shows, many people seek Josh out for advice, making him more central to the network than Lukas and thus highly influential.

Formal hierarchy

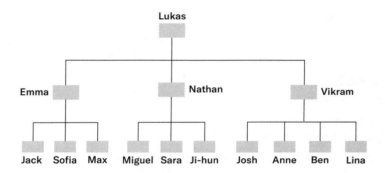

Informal network

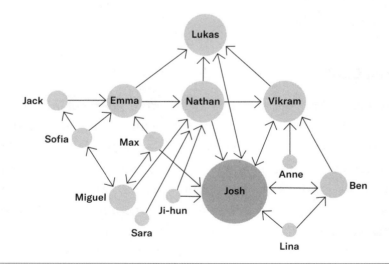

network centrality is critical to success, whether you're a middle manager or a high-ranking boss.

Consider John, one of the NHS change agents we studied. He wanted to set up a nurse-led preoperative assessment service that would free up time for the doctors who previously led the assessments, reduce cancelled operations (and costs), and improve patient care. Although John was a senior doctor, near the top of the hospital's formal hierarchy, he had joined the organization less than a year earlier and was not yet well connected internally. As he started talking to other doctors and to nurses about the change, he encountered a lot of resistance. He was about to give up when Carol, a well-respected nurse, offered to help. She had much less seniority than John, but many colleagues relied on her advice about navigating hospital politics. She knew many of the people whose support John needed, and she eventually converted them to the change.

Another example comes from Gustaf, an equity partner at a U.S. law firm, and Penny, his associate. Gustaf was trying to create a client-file transfer system to ensure continuity in client service during lawyers' absences. But his seniority was no help in getting other lawyers to support the initiative; they balked at the added coordination the system required. That all changed when Penny took on the project. Because colleagues frequently sought her out for advice and respected her judgment, making her central to the company's informal network, she quickly succeeded in persuading people to adopt the new system. She reached out to stakeholders individually, with both substantive and personal arguments. Because they liked her and saw her as knowledgeable and authentic, they listened to her.

It's no shock that centrally positioned people like Carol and Penny make successful change agents; we know that informal connections give people access to information, knowledge, opportunities, and personal support, and thus the ability to mobilize others. But we were surprised in our research by how little formal authority mattered relative to network centrality; among the middle and senior managers we studied, high rank did not improve the odds that their changes would be adopted. That's not to say hierarchy isn't important—in most organizations it is. But our findings indicate that people at any level who wish to exert influence as change agents should be central to the organization's informal network.

The Shape of Your Network Matters

Network position matters. But so does network type. In a *cohesive network*, the people you are connected to are connected to one another. This can be advantageous because social cohesion leads to high levels of trust and support. Information and ideas are corroborated through multiple channels, maximizing understanding, so it's easier to coordinate the group. And people are more likely to be consistent in their words and deeds since they know that discrepancies will be spotted. In a *bridging network*, by contrast, you are connected to people who aren't connected to one another. There are benefits to that, too, because you get access to novel information and knowledge instead of hearing the same things over and over again. You control when and how you pass information along. And you can adapt your message for different people in the network because they're unlikely to talk to one another. The exhibit below shows both types of networks.

Which type of network is better for implementing change? The answer is an academic's favorite: It depends. It depends on how much the change causes the organization to diverge from

Cohesive network

The people in your network are connected to one another. This builds trust and mutual support, facilitating communication and coordination.

Bridging network

Your network contacts are not connected to one another. You are the bridge between disparate individuals and groups, giving you control over what, when, and how you communicate with them.

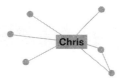

its institutional norms or traditional ways of getting work done, and how much resistance it generates as a result.

Consider, for instance, an NHS attempt to transfer some responsibility for patient discharge from doctors to nurses. This is a *divergent change*: It violates the deeply entrenched role division that gives doctors full authority over such decisions. In the legal profession, a divergent change might be to use a measure other than billable hours to determine compensation. In academia, it might involve the elimination of tenure. Such changes require dramatic shifts in values and practices that have been taken for granted. A *nondivergent change* builds on rather than disrupts existing norms and practices. Many of the NHS initiatives we studied were nondivergent in that they aimed to give even more power to doctors—for example, by putting them in charge of new quality-control systems.

A cohesive network works well when the change is not particularly divergent. Most people in the change agent's network will trust their intentions. Those who are harder to convince will be pressured by others in the network to cooperate and will probably give in because the change is not too disruptive. But for more-dramatic transformations, a bridging network works better—first, because unconnected resisters are less likely to form a coalition; and second, because the change agent can vary the timing and framing of messages for different contacts, highlighting issues that speak to individuals' needs and goals.

Consider, for instance, an NHS nurse who implemented the change in discharge decision authority, described above, in her hospital. She explained how her connections to managers, other nurses, and doctors helped her tailor and time her appeals for each constituency:

> *I first met with the management of the hospital to secure their support. I insisted that nurse-led discharge would help us reduce waiting times for patients, which was one of the key targets that the government had set. I then focused on nurses. I wanted them to understand how important it was to increase their voice in the hospital and to demonstrate how they could contribute to the organizational agenda. Once I had their full support, I turned to doctors. I expected that they would stamp their feet and dig their heels in. To overcome their resistance, I insisted that the new discharge process would reduce their workload, thereby enabling them to focus on complex cases and ensure quicker patient turnover.*

By contrast, another nurse, who led the same initiative at her hospital, admitted that she was handicapped by her cohesive network: Instead of supporting her, the key stakeholders she knew quickly joined forces against the effort. She never overcame their resistance.

The cases of two NHS managers, both of whom had to convince colleagues of the merits of a new computerized booking system (a nondivergent change), are also telling. Martin, who had a cohesive network, succeeded in just a few months because his contacts trusted him and one another, even if they were initially reluctant to make the switch. But Robert, whose bridging network meant that his key contacts weren't connected to one another, struggled for more than six months to build support.

We've observed these patterns in other organizations and industries. Sanjay, the CTO of a software company, wanted his R&D department to embrace open innovation and collaborate with outside groups rather than work strictly in-house, as it had always done. Since joining the company four years earlier, Sanjay had developed relationships with people in various siloed departments. His bridging network allowed him to tailor his proposal to each audience. For the CFO, he emphasized lower product development costs; for the VP of sales, the ability to reduce development time and adapt more quickly to client needs; for the marketing director, the resources that could flow into his department; for his own team, a chance to outsource some R&D and focus only on the most enriching projects.

Change agents must be sure that the shape of their networks suits the type of change they want to pursue. If there's a mismatch, they can enlist people with not just the right skills and competencies but also the right kind of network to act on their behalf. We have seen executives use this approach very successfully

> ## Diagnose Your Network
>
> ### How central am I in my organization's informal network?
>
> Ask yourself: "Do people come to me for work-related advice?" When colleagues rely on you, it signals that they trust you and respect your competence, wisdom, and influence.
>
> ### Do I have a cohesive or a bridging network?
>
> Ask yourself: "Are my network contacts connected to one another?" You may not be able to answer this question with 100% accuracy, but it is worth investigating. Your network type can affect your success.
>
> ### Which influential fence-sitters and resisters am I close to?
>
> Ask yourself: "Who in my network is ambivalent about a proposed change and who is strongly opposed to it?" If it's not obvious where your contacts stand, use the OAR principle—observe, analyze, record—to sort them into groups. Pay attention to how people behave; ask questions, both direct and indirect, to gauge their sentiments; and keep a mental record of your observations. Research shows that managers can learn to map the networks around them—and network insight is, in itself, a source of power.

by appointing a change initiative "cochair" whose relationships offer a better fit.

Keep Fence-Sitters Close and Beware of Resisters

We know from past research that identifying influential people who can convert others is crucial for successful change. Organizations generally include three types of people who can enable or block an initiative: *endorsers*, who are positive about the change; *resisters*, who take a purely negative view; and *fence-sitters*, who see both potential benefits and potential drawbacks.

Which of these people should change agents be close to—that is, share a personal relationship built on mutual trust, liking, and a sense of social obligation? Should they follow the old adage "Keep your friends close and your enemies closer"? Or focus, as politicians often do, on the swing voters, assuming that the resisters are a lost cause? These questions are important; change initiatives deplete both energy and time, so you have to choose your battles.

Again, our research indicates that the answers often depend on the type of change. We found that being close to endorsers has no impact on the success of either divergent or nondivergent change. Of course, identifying champions and enlisting their help is absolutely crucial to your success. But deepening your relationships with them will not make them more engaged and effective. If people like a new idea, they will help enable it whether they are close to you or not. Several NHS change agents we interviewed were surprised to see doctors and nurses they hardly knew become advocates purely because they believed in the initiative.

With fence-sitters, the opposite is true. Being personally close to them can tip their influence in your favor no matter the type of change—they see not only drawbacks but also benefits, and they will be reluctant to disappoint a friend.

As for resisters, there is no universal rule; again, it depends on how divergent the change is and the intensity of the opposition to it. Because resistance is not always overt or even conscious, change agents must watch closely and infer people's attitudes. For nondivergent initiatives, close relationships with resisters

Match your network to the type of change you're pursuing

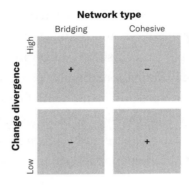

Consider how being close to influencers can affect your success

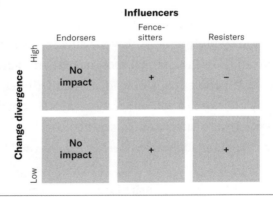

present an opportunity—their sense of social obligation may cause them to rethink the issue. But in the case of divergent change, resisters typically perceive a significant threat and are much less susceptible to social pressure. It's also important to note that the relationship works both ways: Change agents might be reluctant to pursue an initiative that's opposed by people they trust. They might decide that the emotional cost is too high.

An NHS clinical manager who failed in her effort to transfer responsibility for a rehabilitation unit from a physician to a physiotherapist—a divergent change—described her feelings this way: "Some of my colleagues with whom I had worked for a long time continued to oppose the project. Mary, whom I've known forever, thought that it was not a good idea. It was a bit hard on me."

By contrast, a doctor who launched the same initiative in her organization did not try to convert resisters but instead focused on fence-sitters. This strategy was effective. As one of her initially ambivalent colleagues explained, "She came to me early on and asked me to support her. I know her well, and I like her. I could not be one of the people who would prevent her from succeeding."

Similarly, John, a member of the operating committee of a boutique investment bank, initiated a rebalancing of traditional end-of-year compensation with a deferred component that linked pay to longer-term performance—a particularly divergent change in small banks that rely on annual bonus schemes to attract talent. His close relationships with several fence-sitters enabled him to turn them into proponents. He also heard out the resisters in his network. But having concluded that the change was needed, he maintained his focus by keeping them at a distance until the new system had the green light.

The important point is to be mindful of your relationships with influencers. Being close to endorsers certainly won't hurt, but it won't make them more engaged, either. Fence-sitters can always help, so make time to take them out to lunch, express an authentic interest in their opinions, and find similarities with them in order to build goodwill and common purpose. Handle resisters with care: If you're pursuing a disruptive initiative, you probably won't change their mind—but they might change yours. By all means, hear them out in order to understand their opposition; the change

> ## How We Conducted the Study
>
> Our findings are based on in-depth studies of 68 change initiatives over 12 months at the UK's National Health Service (NHS). We began by mapping the formal rank and informal networks of the middle and senior clinical managers spearheading the changes. Data on their demographics, position, and professional trajectories came from their curriculum vitae and NHS human resource records, while informal network data came from surveys, field visits, and interviews with them and their colleagues. We then gathered data about the content and adoption rates of the initiatives through field visits, interviews, telephone surveys conducted 12 months after implementation, and qualitative assessments from colleagues who had either collaborated with the change agents or observed them in the workplace.

you're pursuing may in fact be wrongheaded. But if you're still convinced of its importance, keep resisters at arm's length. All three of our findings underscore the importance of networks in influencing change. First, formal authority may give you the illusion of power, but informal networks always matter, whether you are the boss or a middle manager. Second, think about what kind of network you have—or your appointed change agent has—and make sure it matches the type of change you're after. A bridging network helps drive divergent change; a cohesive network is preferable for nondivergent change. Third, always identify and cultivate fence-sitters, but handle resisters on a case-by-case basis. We saw clear evidence that these three network factors dramatically improved NHS managers' odds of successfully implementing all kinds of reforms. We believe they can do the same for change agents in a wide variety of organizations.

Originally published in July–August 2013. Reprint R1307D

7

What Everyone Gets Wrong About Change Management

by N. Anand and Jean-Louis Barsoux

Corporate transformations still have a miserable success rate, even though scholars and consultants have significantly improved our understanding of how they work. Studies consistently report that about three-quarters of change efforts flop—either they fail to deliver the anticipated benefits or they are abandoned entirely.

Because flawed implementation is most often blamed for such failures, organizations have focused on improving execution. They have embraced the idea that transformation is a process with key stages that must be carefully managed and levers that must be pulled—indeed, expressions such as "burning platform," "guiding coalition," and "quick wins" are now common in the change management lexicon. But poor execution is only part of the problem; our analysis suggests that misdiagnosis is equally to blame. Often organizations pursue the wrong changes—especially in complex and fast-moving environments, where decisions about what to transform in order to remain competitive can be hasty or misguided.

Before worrying about *how* to change, executive teams need to figure out *what* to change—in particular, what to change *first*. That's the challenge we set out to investigate in our four-year study of 62 corporate transformations.

When companies don't choose their transformation battles wisely, their efforts have a negative effect on performance. Consider what happened after Ron Johnson took over as CEO of J.C. Penney: He immediately gave store design and pricing an overhaul to attract younger, trendier customers. Sales sank by a quarter, and the stock plummeted by half.

Johnson's first priority should have been a better integration of JCP's in-store and online operations. At that time customers could not find in the stores what was being showcased online, and vice versa. The two channels were run separately, each with its own merchandise and supply chain. Johnson's eventual replacement, Marvin Ellison, recognized the misalignment and restored JCP to profitability. Under Ellison's leadership, JCP became nimbler and more responsive to customers looking for deals (who had left in droves because of Johnson's changes). The retailer redesigned its shopping app to make it easier for in-store customers to find discounts, improved its website, and caught up with rivals by offering same-day in-store pickup of items ordered online.

As JCP and many other companies have learned, the costs of setting off on the wrong transformation journey are significant: First, underlying problems will persist and worsen as attention is invested elsewhere (JCP fell further behind in online

Idea in Brief

The Problem
Failed corporate transformations are usually attributed to execution—but often leaders misdiagnose what changes need to be made.

The Costs
When organizations pursue the wrong changes or tackle them in the wrong order, existing problems get worse, new ones are created, and employees, having been burned, become wary of future initiatives.

The Solution
Before setting their change priorities, leaders should analyze three things: the catalyst for transformation, the underlying quest, and the leadership capabilities needed to pursue it.

---

sales as it freshened up store design). Second, new problems may emerge (JCP alienated loyal, deal-driven customers with its new pricing strategy and saddled itself with more than $5 billion of debt, which hampered its ability to invest in technology). And third, the executive team risks undermining employee commitment to future initiatives (Ellison had to remobilize a workforce still traumatized by JCP's near collapse under Johnson). Having "fixed the plumbing," Ellison's leadership team has turned its attention to making JCP more relevant to shoppers in the coming decade. Although it has averted disaster, the company still has a lot of work to do. After a rough holiday season in 2016, the executive team decided to close almost 140 stores to compete more effectively with online retailers. The need for transformation is ongoing.

So how can leaders decide which changes to prioritize at the moment? By fully understanding three things: the catalyst for transformation, the organization's underlying quest, and the leadership capabilities needed to see it through. Our analysis of stalled transformations suggests that failing to examine and align these factors drastically reduces the odds of producing lasting change. In this article we illustrate this dynamic with several classic case studies that provide enough distance to observe and compare clear, verifiable outcomes. We also offer tools to help diagnose what's needed in your company's transformation efforts.

The Catalyst: Pursuing Value

The trigger for any corporate transformation is the pursuit of value. Ideally, that entails both improving efficiency (through streamlining and cost cutting) and reinvesting in growth. But many transformation efforts derail because they focus too narrowly on one or the other.

In some cases, attempts to streamline the business through productivity improvements, outsourcing, divestments, or restructuring undermine growth. The cuts are so deep that they hollow out capabilities, sap morale, and remove the slack that could have fueled new endeavors.

Consider Norske Skog, once the world's largest newsprint producer—now, according to Bloomberg, the third largest in Europe, in a dwindling market. Hit by falling demand for paper more than a decade ago, the Norwegian company was forced to divest unprofitable operations across four continents. Thanks to its profitability improvement program, it became so good at identifying where to make cuts that it was praised by *BusinessWeek* in 2009 for turning "shrinking into a science." But although the company has survived, it has not found a way to rebound. Like many companies in contracting or commoditizing industries, it is stuck in turnaround mode, with its share price consistently in decline. By contrast, its Swedish-Finnish paper rival Stora Enso also went through several rounds of painful restructuring but has since reinvented itself as a renewable-materials company.

In other cases, reinvestment in growth spins out of control. Lego had this problem. The Danish toy maker made two large-scale attempts to transform itself through greater innovation. The first, launched in 2000, delivered a wealth of freewheeling experimentation that over the next few years drove the company to the brink of bankruptcy. The second, launched in 2006 (once the company had recovered its financial stability), catapulted Lego past the two U.S. giants Hasbro and Mattel to become the world's most profitable toy company by 2014, with margins greater than 30%. Why the big difference? The second time around, under then CEO Jørgen Vig Knudstorp, Lego maintained a dual focus on growth *and* discipline. The company set up a cross-functional committee (the Executive Innovation Governance Group) to fund, monitor, and strategically coordinate innovation activities, ensuring that they remained "around the box" rather than drifting way outside it.

This example brings us to a larger point about catalysts for change: While you're striving for growth, discipline—through governance, metrics, and other controls—allows you to stay on track later on, after you have chosen your journey's direction. Without such controls in place, your company can easily lose its way. This often happens through the hasty purchase of an overpriced or tough-to-integrate "transformative acquisition" that is meant to redirect the strategy but just ends up sucking value out of the corporation. Hewlett-Packard is a notable recidivist in this domain: Recall its ill-fated acquisitions of Compaq, EDS, and Autonomy.

But how can you and others on the leadership team figure out what kind of transformation to pursue, once growth opportunities or declining performance has alerted you to the need for major change of some kind? That's the second step in the process—defining the quest.

The Quest: Choosing Your Direction

Next the organization must identify the specific quest that will lead to greater value generation. Executives increasingly use the term "transformation" as shorthand for "digital transformation." But the ongoing digital revolution does not itself constitute a transformation—it is a means to an end, and you must define what that end should be.

Studies and analysis that we have conducted show that most corporate transformation efforts are either derivatives or combinations of five prototypical quests:

1. *Global presence:* extending market reach and becoming more international in terms of leadership, innovation, talent flows, capabilities, and best practices

2. *Customer focus:* understanding your customers' needs and providing enhanced insights, experiences, or outcomes (integrated solutions) rather than just products or services

3. *Nimbleness:* accelerating processes or simplifying how work gets done to become more strategically, operationally, and culturally agile

4. *Innovation:* incorporating ideas and approaches from fresh sources, both internal and external, to expand the organization's options for exploiting new opportunities

5. *Sustainability:* becoming greener and more socially responsible in positioning and execution

What Everyone Gets Wrong About Change Management

Understanding the five quests

The best execution in the world won't lead to a successful transformation if your organization pursues the wrong change. Quests fall into five categories, and more than one may be relevant, so leadership teams must decide which to prioritize and which to postpone. Pursuing too many quests at once is a recipe for failure.

Quest	Enablers	Blockers
Global presence Become more international in mindset as well as market reach by *reconfiguring the operating model*	• Rewiring systems and networks to leverage capabilities, knowledge, and ideas wherever they are • Preserving corporate principles while remaining flexible on cultural practices • Using diversity as a source of competitive advantage	• Acquiring weak businesses in haste to develop a global footprint • Honoring the "dominant" culture while paying lip service to the rest • Failing to integrate talent on a global scale
Customer focus Provide tailored solutions to user problems by *reconfiguring the customer experience*	• Organizing, equipping, training, and rewarding the workforce to better understand and address customers' needs • Redefining relationships with vendors, intermediaries, and suppliers • Reframing customer relations to learn rather than simply to close deals	• Failing to reshape an entrenched culture that emphasizes pushing products • Continuing to depend on former sales intermediaries • Not coordinating front- and back-office units to deliver seamless solutions
Innovation Tap multiple sources of ideas and approaches by *reconfiguring R&D partners*	• Navigating the full innovation spectrum, from value chain partners to competitors to lead users and crowdsourcing • Collaborating to convert new ideas into tangible innovation • Articulating innovation needs clearly and creating win-win outcomes with partners	• Relying too much on one or two parts of the innovation spectrum • Resorting to rigid contracts with innovation partners • Lacking oversight that ensures frugal investment

(continued)

Understanding the five quests (continued)

Quest	Enablers	Blockers
Nimbleness Become more strategically, operationally, and culturally agile by *reconfiguring business processes*	• Developing the capability to detect and respond to major changes in the environment • Leveraging diversity to exploit opportunities • Learning to prototype rapidly and institutionalizing what works	• Allowing blind spots to produce an incomplete picture • Responding too slowly because of red tape • Taking too long to cut your losses when something doesn't work
Sustainability Become greener and more socially responsible by *reconfiguring resources*	• Engaging all stakeholders to become sustainable • Leveraging sustainability as a source of strategic advantage • Communicating top-team commitment to the sustainability agenda	• Undermeasuring or underreporting progress toward sustainability • Broadcasting shallow PR victories ("greenwashing") • Failing to balance efficiency and sustainability goals

Each quest has its own focus, enablers, and derailers, and each requires the company to do something more or different with its operating model, customers, partners, internal processes, or resources. "Going digital" can support any of the five quests, and all of them call for discipline.

Let's return to the paper giant Stora Enso to see how it defined its quest. The catalyst for transformation was the plunging demand for paper along with the rise of digitization. Stora desperately needed not only to cut costs but also to rethink its business focus.

Members of the top team consulted widely with various divisions and layers of the company and engaged in lengthy deliberations. Weighing the options, they concluded that pursuing nimbleness, global presence, or customer focus would merely yield more market share in a declining industry. Innovation would not solve the main issue either. But the company had developed some breakthrough green offerings, including environmentally friendly packaging for the expanding e-commerce delivery market. Its greatest opportunity lay in shifting the whole axis of the business to specialize in offerings made with renewable and bio-based materials. So Stora's was a sustainability quest. That turned out to be a shrewd pivot. Traditional paper-based products now represent only 8% of Stora's profits, and the company's share price has almost tripled since November 2011.

It can be difficult to choose the right quest. Should the company expand into new regions, get closer to customers, innovate with more partners, get faster and more responsive, or become more sustainable? Executives sometimes say "all of the above"—but that's too much to handle at once. The right quest should be a compelling and uncontested priority. In some of the cases we analyzed, companies straddled quests (customer focus and agility, for instance, or innovation and sustainability). That can work as long as the components are fused into one cogent focus.

With multiple organizational challenges jostling for attention, top teams are liable to disagree on the transformation priority. That's why we created a 15-question audit. In our research and consulting engagements, we've found that this tool allows executives to do their own systematic review so that they can make smart decisions regarding transformation. For example, at a French utility company we worked with, the top 200 executives participated in a "transformation jam" where they all filled out a status report that identified the critical enablers and blockers for each potential quest. This and the quest audit helped to clarify and reconcile the priorities of different parts of the organization, from the boardroom and the C-suite to the front lines.

Conduct a Quest Audit

Rate each of these competencies on a 1-to-7 scale (7 is strongest). Your lowest scores will identify your most urgent priorities for change.

Global Presence

How well do we...

- pursue expansion with a strategic global perspective?
- share local learning about business practices globally?
- use digital technology to bring together key populations?

Customer Focus

How well do we...

- create offerings with meaningful value to customers?
- recognize team-based efforts in developing and selling solutions?
- use analytics to identify which solutions customers need most?

Innovation

How well do we...

- cooperate with external partners to create new technologies and offerings?
- create an environment of trust for effective collaboration?
- leverage digital platforms for innovation?

Nimbleness

How well do we...

- sense changes in the environment?
- act on those changes in a timely way?
- share information across the organization?

> **Sustainability**
>
> How well do we...
>
> - integrate our sustainability strategy into the overall corporate vision and strategy?
> - implement sustainability in decision-making, processes, and systems throughout the organization?
> - use digital technology to catalog and evaluate sustainability initiatives?

The Capabilities: Developing Leaders

Finally, to support the chosen quest, the company must develop leaders who can see it through. Sustained transformation depends on this.

Again Stora Enso is a useful case in point. Jouko Karvinen, the company's CEO until July 2014, realized that his executive team—all Nordics, all industry veterans—could continue to squeeze costs out of core businesses but would struggle to explore prospects for fresh growth. So, in close consultation with then HR head Lars Häggström, he set up a parallel "Pathfinders" leadership team—a dozen managers from various parts of the organization—and gave them a mandate to identify sustainability opportunities that were falling between silos and, more broadly, to challenge the old ways of doing business. Each year the organization replaces its Pathfinders with a new cohort of up to 16 members. At first this was mainly a way to keep bringing new perspectives into high-level decision-making, but it expanded into a program for identifying and developing change agents within the organization who would then serve as internal management consultants. The Pathfinders program became the centerpiece of the company's new leadership-development activities.

Transformation journeys run out of steam when companies neglect leadership development. In order to keep an organization moving in the desired direction, executives and managers at all levels must understand which mindsets and behaviors will take the company there and then take care to model them so that employees know how to act in the new context.

Any mismatch between the leadership-development effort and the transformation quest is bound to impair value generation. The need for alignment is well demonstrated by the familiar but instructive story of two Asian rivals in personal computing.

In 2008 Taiwan's Acer and China's Lenovo ranked third and fourth respectively in global market share, well behind HP and Dell. By 2015 Lenovo had claimed the top spot and Acer had slipped to sixth. They had defined similar quests—achieving global reach—and they pursued similar strategies, seizing opportunities to generate value and transform their global presence by acquiring embattled Western businesses. Lenovo grabbed IBM's PC division in 2005; Acer snapped up Gateway in the United States in 2007 and Packard Bell in Europe in 2008. But a key difference between Lenovo and Acer was their commitment to globalizing the senior leadership ranks.

Acer's board struggled with "de-Taiwanization," rejecting CEO Gianfranco Lanci's bold plans to hire foreign talent with expertise in mobile technology and to triple the number of engineers. (It's worth noting that Lanci soon left Acer to head up Lenovo's PC group.) In 2010 Acer had six foreigners among its top 24 executives; by 2014 it was down to three out of 23. In the same period, the board went from having two foreign directors to having none. Predictably, the top team's decision-making became increasingly cautious and inward-looking. In 2016, for example, it hired the founder's son to head up the company's cloud services, which prompted the *TechNews* headline "Is Acer Becoming a Family Business?"

By contrast, leadership development at Lenovo was fully in line with the company's quest for a greater global presence. By 2012 its top team of nine represented six nationalities. Its Chinese CEO, Yang Yuanqing, relocated to the United States, and other members of the team were scattered globally, gathering for one week each month in a different strategic market. Aware of the challenges his team faced as a result of its members' varied backgrounds, the CEO brought in a coach to work with the executives on cross-cultural issues. And to promote diversity as a source of competitive advantage—in both hiring and operations companywide—Lenovo elevated the role of cultural integration and diversity VP to the C-suite. Such efforts paved the way for ambitious acquisitions and joint ventures with German, Japanese, Brazilian, and U.S. companies—enabling Lenovo to extend into new software and services categories globally.

Transformation Traps

Many transformation efforts are set up to fail at the quest stage. Top teams get sidetracked or overreach when they lose focus on what value is worth pursuing—or they take on more change than their leadership capabilities can steer. Our investigations reveal three common failings:

Neglecting the quest

In companies that don't identify a mobilizing theme, value generation and leadership development can become ends in themselves—generic efforts, not really linked to the strategy. For example, India's Infosys developed a widely admired approach to leadership development but ran into trouble because it failed to tie that to the transformational needs of the business—forcing the IT giant to turn to an outside CEO to drive the necessary changes.

Being seduced by the wrong quest

The board and the top team may be led astray by the vision of a forceful CEO (like Ron Johnson at J.C. Penney), try to copy the strategic moves of competitors, or fall for recommendations from consultants who favor particular quests. In those situations, the chosen quest misfires because it was not the product of deep deliberation or shared conviction or it fails to address the central issue. For example, GE transplant Bob Nardelli tried to transform Home Depot by selling supplies to construction professionals as well as to homeowners. The pursuit of customers in adjacent markets distracted attention from Home Depot's core problem of slumping store sales. When Nardelli resigned, under intense pressure from shareholders, the strategy was immediately reversed and the wholesale arm sold off to allow the company to refocus on its core retail business. From seventh-largest global retailer, Home Depot has since jumped to third.

Focusing on multiple quests

The quest choice may be muddled if leaders can't agree on which direction to go. Different parts of the business (regions, functions, levels) see different problems and priorities. Some corporations overreach, taking on too many quests at once or overestimating their leadership capabilities in a given area. Back in 2009 the incoming Carrefour CEO, Lars Olofsson, launched an ambitious transformation plan for the retail giant based on seven strategic initiatives, including enhanced innovation, customer engagement, agility, and global expansion. The result was confusion, a loss of domestic market share, and a 53% plunge in share price in one year. Olofsson lasted barely two years in the job. His replacement, Georges Plassat, panned the leadership capability of the previous team, labeling the members "incompetent in mass retailing." In a successful recovery plan, Plassat first focused on shedding operations in noncore markets and streamlining internal operations. He then reignited domestic sales by cutting prices and diversifying stores. Three years later Carrefour had regained a clear lead in the French market.

Getting Started

It can be useful to think of value generation and leadership development as the chariot wheels that support a transformation, and the quest as the horse that provides direction and momentum. Alignment among the three is critical if you want to reach your destination.

The quest audit facilitates alignment by making it easier to diagnose the current situation, identify which transformation could be a game changer, and decide which enablers and blockers to target to make it happen. This tool has been validated with more than 500 executives and road tested by a dozen companies (across industries and continents) seeking to transform themselves. It helps address these underlying challenges:

Facing reality

Having a structured way to solicit and gather input allows senior teams to take a cold, hard look at the company. Knowledge, competencies, or activities that were once central to the organization may have become what Harvard's Dorothy Leonard-Barton calls core rigidities. If so, they need to be adapted or jettisoned. The more radical the transformation, the greater the chance that such limitations will be exposed. Confronting harsh reality may also involve identifying and addressing blind spots.

For the HR head of a European postal services group, a quest audit revealed a disconcerting pattern. "The low scores on value, customer focus, and innovation seem to highlight our company's ineffectiveness in listening respectively to the market, to our customers, and to suppliers or partners," she told her team. "It's hard to admit, but it's better to recognize now the inertia of our organization that needs to be tackled urgently." Similarly, the head of HR at a Japanese food group observed that doing the exercise opened up team dialogue on issues that were previously off-limits: "It provided 'permission' to reflect on the current reality and how we got to where we are. That immunity led us to frame some breakthrough questions to understand our challenge and what we needed to do to solve it."

Debating priorities

Often the diagnosis reveals multiple challenges and the debate centers on which of them matters most—or which can be tackled immediately, given the company's current leadership capabilities. Conceptual tools can't tell top teams what to do, but they can support a smarter discussion, with much of the critical information visible at a glance.

By mapping out where various parties see opportunities and hazards, executives can avoid a major decision-making trap: getting stuck with a false choice between pursuing one strategic option and doing nothing. Articulating the pressures and challenges makes it easier to debate and evaluate the relative merits of various responses.

Take the case of Cosentino, a Spanish manufacturer of engineered surfaces for kitchens and bathrooms. Because the company had established a solid distribution foothold in the United States, the most obvious strategy was to keep extending its global presence. But after using the quest audit to weigh their options, the top 70 executives decided instead to prioritize co-innovation—not just with Cosentino's supply chain partners but with other high-end kitchen and bathroom businesses (facades, flooring, and equipment)—to anticipate new trends. They elected to work on their biggest weakness rather than to build on an obvious strength.

Reconciling perspectives or priorities and developing a shared understanding of the cause of the current state of affairs is not painless. But sidestepping that discomfort only reduces the chances of selecting a viable transformation objective. According to the head of finance of an Italian fashion group, "Our discussions highlighted areas where we perhaps were not as aligned as we thought and emphasized common pain points regardless of where you sit in the organization. The reflection drove convergence about what we needed to do and stop doing."

Joint consultation also builds a sense of involvement that boosts the perception of fair process and therefore commitment to the chosen course of action.

Communicating choices

Having debated the priorities and challenges, an organization's leaders can feel more confident in advocating a particular course of action and communicating the message to others. They are better equipped to explain how they reached this conclusion, what alternatives they scrutinized, and why they think this is the right transformation journey. If employees feel that the analytical work was thorough and inclusive, they are more likely to accept the decision, even if they don't like it.

Of course, analysis alone seldom inspires people to act in unfamiliar and perhaps unwelcome ways. When leading people into an uncertain future, it helps if the decision-makers can get people talking about enablers and blockers. That gives everyone a sense of where the organization stands, what it must transform—and why, beyond "survival," the journey is worth making.

Here's an example of how this can play out: At GroupM, the world's largest media investment group, the top team of the South Asia operation concluded that its competition in the digital age consisted of not just the traditional agency networks but also disruptive startups and digital platforms that could cultivate direct access to its clients. As the team debated priorities, innovation through deeper partnerships with potential new competitors emerged as number one. Further discussions, including one mediated by a "youth committee" made up of highfliers under the age of 30, revealed that a key enabler was the ability to pick the right innovation partners. A key blocker, according to C. V. L. Srinivas, the division's CEO, was "getting people working in a successful organization to change their mindset and accept that we needed to change in order to stay relevant." So the top team chose a communication strategy that balanced hard and soft approaches: setting tough targets for employees to increase their proportion of digital work while making it clear that they would receive the support and training to achieve those goals.

Conclusion

As the shelf life of business strategies grows shorter, a corporation's transformation capability becomes its only enduring advantage. A quest for innovation provided a focus for Lego's transformation under Knudstorp. But now, as Lego nears saturation in its lead markets, such as the United States and Germany, its attention is on fast-growth emerging economies—the new quest being to transform a Danish brand with global appeal into a truly global corporation.

With serial transformations becoming the norm, a key strategic question for any corporate leader is, How can we make our next transformation flourish? This article will help you answer that question.

Originally published in November–December 2017. Reprint R1706D

A Survival Guide for Leaders

by Ronald Heifetz and Marty Linsky

Think of the many top executives in recent years who, sometimes after long periods of considerable success, have crashed and burned. Or think of individuals you have known in less prominent positions, perhaps people spearheading significant change initiatives in their organizations, who have suddenly found themselves out of a job. Think about yourself: In exercising leadership, have *you* ever been removed or pushed aside?

Let's face it, to lead is to live dangerously. While leadership is often depicted as an exciting and glamorous endeavor, one in which you inspire others to follow you through good times and bad, such a portrayal ignores leadership's dark side: the inevitable attempts to take you out of the game.

Those attempts are sometimes justified. People in top positions must often pay the price for a flawed strategy or a series of bad decisions. But frequently, something more is at work. We're not talking here about conventional office politics; we're talking about the high-stake risks you face whenever you try to lead an organization through difficult but necessary change. The risks during such times are especially high because change that truly transforms an organization, be it a multibillion-dollar company or a 10-person sales team, demands that people give up things they hold dear: daily habits, loyalties, ways of thinking. In return for these sacrifices, they may be offered nothing more than the possibility of a better future.

We refer to this kind of wrenching organizational transformation as "adaptive change," something very different from the "technical change" that occupies people in positions of authority on a regular basis. Technical problems, while often challenging, can be solved applying existing know-how and the organization's current problem-solving processes. Adaptive problems resist these kinds of solutions because they require individuals throughout the organization to alter their ways; as the people themselves are the problem, the solution lies with them. (See the sidebar "Adaptive Versus Technical Change: Whose Problem Is It?") Responding to an adaptive challenge with a technical fix may have some short-term appeal. But to make real progress, sooner or later those who lead must ask themselves and the people in the organization to face a set of deeper issues—and to accept a solution that may require turning part or all of the organization upside down.

It is at this point that danger lurks. And most people who lead in such a situation—swept up in the action, championing a cause they believe in—are caught unawares. Over and over again, we have seen courageous souls blissfully ignorant of an approaching threat until it was too late to respond.

Idea in Brief

It's exciting—even glamorous—to lead others through good times and bad. But leadership also has its dark side: the inevitable attempts to take you out of the game when you're steering your organization through difficult change.

Leading change requires asking people to confront painful issues and give up habits and beliefs they hold dear. Result? Some people try to eliminate change's visible agent—you. Whether they attack you personally, undermine your authority, or seduce you into seeing things their way, their goal is the same: to derail you, easing their pain and restoring familiar order.

How to resist attempts to remove you—and continue to propel change forward? Manage your hostile environment—your organization and its people—and your own vulnerabilities.

The hazard can take numerous forms. You may be attacked directly in an attempt to shift the debate to your character and style and avoid discussion of your initiative. You may be marginalized, forced into the position of becoming so identified with one issue that your broad authority is undermined. You may be seduced by your supporters and, fearful of losing their approval and affection, fail to demand they make the sacrifices needed for the initiative to succeed. You may be diverted from your goal by people overwhelming you with the day-to-day details of carrying it out, keeping you busy and preoccupied.

Each one of these thwarting tactics—whether done consciously or not—grows out of people's aversion to the organizational disequilibrium created by your initiative. By attempting to undercut you, people strive to restore order, maintain what is familiar to them, and protect themselves from the pains of adaptive change. They want to be comfortable again, and you're in the way.

Adaptive Versus Technical Change: Whose Problem Is It?

The importance—and difficulty—of distinguishing between adaptive and technical change can be illustrated with an analogy. When your car has problems, you go to a mechanic. Most of the time, the mechanic can fix the car. But if your car troubles stem from the way a family member drives, the problems are likely to recur. Treating the problems as purely technical ones—taking the car to the mechanic time and again to get it back on the road—masks the real issues. Maybe you need to get your mother to stop drinking and driving, get your grandfather to give up his driver's license, or get your teenager to be more cautious. Whatever the underlying problems, the mechanic can't solve them. Instead, changes in the family need to occur, and that won't be easy. People will resist the moves, even denying that such problems exist. That's because even those not directly affected by an adaptive change typically experience discomfort when someone upsets a group's or an organization's equilibrium.

Such resistance to adaptive change certainly happens in business. Indeed, it's the classic error: Companies treat adaptive challenges as if they were technical problems. For example, executives attempt to improve the bottom line by cutting costs across the board. Not only does this avoid the need to make tough choices about which areas should be trimmed, it also masks the fact that the company's real challenge lies in redesigning its strategy.

Treating adaptive challenges as technical ones permits executives to do what they have excelled at throughout their careers: solve other people's problems. And it allows others in the organization to enjoy the primordial peace of mind that comes from knowing that their commanding officer has a plan to maintain order and stability. After all, the executive doesn't have to instigate—and the people don't have to undergo—uncomfortable change. Most people would agree that, despite the selective pain of a cost-cutting exercise, it is less traumatic than reinventing a company.

So how do you protect yourself? Over a combined 50 years of teaching and consulting, we have asked ourselves that question time and again—usually while watching top-notch and well-intentioned folks get taken out of the game. On occasion, the question has become painfully personal; we as individuals have been knocked off course or out of the action more than once in our own leadership efforts. So we are offering what we hope are some pragmatic answers that grow out of these observations and experiences. We should note that while our advice clearly applies to senior executives, it also applies to people trying to lead change initiatives from positions of little or no formal organizational authority.

This "survival guide" has two main parts. The first looks outward, offering tactical advice about relating to your organization and the people in it. It is designed to protect you from those trying to push you aside before you complete your initiative. The second looks inward, focusing on your own human needs and vulnerabilities. It is designed to keep you from bringing yourself down.

A Hostile Environment

Leading major organizational change often involves radically reconfiguring a complex network of people, tasks, and institutions that have achieved a kind of modus vivendi, no matter how dysfunctional it appears to you. When the status quo is upset, people feel a sense of profound loss and dashed expectations. They may go through a period of feeling incompetent or disloyal. It's no wonder they resist the change or try to eliminate its visible agent. We offer here a number of techniques—relatively straightforward in concept but difficult to execute—for minimizing these external threats.

Operate in and above the fray

The ability to maintain perspective in the midst of action is critical to lowering resistance. Any military officer knows the importance of maintaining the capacity for reflection, especially in the "fog of war." Great athletes must simultaneously play the game and observe it as a whole. We call this skill "getting off the dance floor and going to the balcony," an image that captures the mental activity of stepping back from the action and asking, "What's really going on here?"

Leadership is an improvisational art. You may be guided by an overarching vision, clear values, and a strategic plan, but what you actually do from moment to moment cannot be scripted. You must respond as events unfold. To use our metaphor, you have to move back and forth from the balcony to the dance floor, over and over again throughout the days, weeks, months, and years. While today's plan may make sense now, tomorrow you'll discover the unanticipated effects of today's actions and have to adjust accordingly. Sustaining good leadership, then, requires first and foremost the capacity to see what is happening to you and your initiative as it is happening and to understand how today's turns in the road will affect tomorrow's plans.

But taking a balcony perspective is extremely tough to do when you're fiercely engaged down below, being pushed and pulled by the events and people around you—and doing some pushing and pulling of your own. Even if you are able to break away, the practice of stepping back and seeing the big picture is complicated by several factors. For example, when you get some distance, you still must accurately interpret what you see and hear. This is easier said than done. In an attempt to avoid difficult change, people will naturally, even unconsciously, defend their habits and ways of thinking. As you seek input from a broad range of people, you'll constantly need to be aware of these hidden agendas. You'll also need to observe your own actions; seeing yourself objectively as you look down from the balcony is perhaps the hardest task of all.

Fortunately, you can learn to be both an observer and a participant at the same time. When you are sitting in a meeting, practice by watching what is happening while it is happening—even as you are part of what is happening. Observe the relationships and see how people's attention to one another can vary: supporting, thwarting, or listening. Watch people's body language. When you make a point, resist the instinct to stay perched on the edge of your seat, ready to defend what you said. A technique as simple as pushing your chair a few inches away from the table after you speak may provide the literal as well as metaphorical distance you need to become an observer.

Court the uncommitted

It's tempting to go it alone when leading a change initiative. There's no one to dilute your ideas or share the glory, and it's often just plain exciting. It's also foolish. You need to recruit partners, people who can help protect you from attacks and who can point out potentially fatal flaws in your strategy or initiative. Moreover, you are far less vulnerable when you are out on the point with a bunch of folks rather than alone. You also need to keep the opposition close. Knowing what your opponents are thinking can help you challenge them more effectively and thwart their attempts to upset your agenda—or allow you to borrow ideas that will improve your initiative. Have coffee once a week with the person most dedicated to seeing you fail.

But while relationships with allies and opponents are essential, the people who will determine your success are often those in the middle, the uncommitted who nonetheless are wary of your plans. They have no substantive stake in your initiative, but they do have a stake in the comfort, stability, and security of the status quo. They've seen change agents come and go, and they know that your initiative will disrupt their lives and make their futures uncertain. You want to be sure that this general uneasiness doesn't evolve into a move to push you aside.

These people will need to see that your intentions are serious—for example, that you are willing to let go of those who can't make the changes your initiative requires. But people must also see that you understand the loss you are asking them to accept. You need to name the loss, be it a change in time-honored work routines or an overhaul of the company's core values, and explicitly acknowledge the resulting pain. You might do this through a series of simple statements, but it often requires something more tangible and public—recall Franklin Roosevelt's radio "fireside chats" during the Great Depression—to convince people that you truly understand.

Beyond a willingness to accept casualties and acknowledge people's losses, two very personal types of action can defuse potential resistance to you and your initiatives. The first is practicing what you preach. In 1972, Gene Patterson took over as editor of the *St. Petersburg Times*. His mandate was to take the respected regional newspaper to a higher level, enhancing its reputation for fine writing while becoming a fearless and hard-hitting news source. This would require major changes not only in the way the community viewed the newspaper but also in the way *Times* reporters thought about themselves and their roles. Because prominent organizations and individuals would no longer be spared warranted criticism, reporters would sometimes be angrily rebuked by the subjects of articles.

A Survival Guide for Leaders

Several years after Patterson arrived, he attended a party at the home of the paper's foreign editor. Driving home, he pulled up to a red light and scraped the car next to him. The police officer called to the scene charged Patterson with driving under the influence. Patterson phoned Bob Haiman, a veteran *Times* newsman who had just been appointed executive editor, and insisted that a story on his arrest be run. As Haiman recalls, he tried to talk Patterson out of it, arguing that DUI arrests that didn't involve injuries were rarely reported, even when prominent figures were involved. Patterson was adamant, however, and insisted that the story appear on page one.

Patterson, still viewed as somewhat of an outsider at the paper, knew that if he wanted his employees to follow the highest journalistic standards, he would have to display those standards, even when it hurt. Few leaders are called upon to disgrace themselves on the front page of a newspaper. But adopting the behavior you expect from others—whether it be taking a pay cut in tough times or spending a day working next to employees on a reconfigured production line—can be crucial in getting buy-in from people who might try to undermine your initiative.

The second thing you can do to neutralize potential opposition is to acknowledge your own responsibility for whatever problems the organization currently faces. If you have been with the company for some time, whether in a position of senior authority or not, you've likely contributed in some way to the current mess. Even if you are new, you need to identify areas of your own behavior that could stifle the change you hope to make.

In our teaching, training, and consulting, we often ask people to write or talk about a leadership challenge they currently face. Over the years, we have read and heard literally thousands of such challenges. Typically, in the first version of the story, the author is nowhere to be found. The underlying message: "If only other people would shape up, I could make progress here." But by too readily pointing your finger at others, you risk making yourself a target. Remember, you are asking people to move to a place where they are frightened to go. If at the same time you're blaming them for having to go there, they will undoubtedly turn against you.

In the early 1990s, Leslie Wexner, founder and CEO of the Limited, realized the need for major changes at the company, including a significant reduction in the workforce. But his consultant told him that something else had to change: long-standing habits that were at the heart of his self-image. In particular, he had to stop treating the company as if it were his family. The indulgent father had to become the chief personnel officer, putting the right people in the right jobs and holding them accountable for their work. "I was an athlete trained to be a baseball player," Wexner recalled during a recent speech at Harvard's Kennedy School. "And one day, someone tapped me on the shoulder and said, 'Football.' And I said, 'No, I'm a baseball player. 'And he said, 'Football.' And I said, 'I don't know how to play football. I'm not 6'4", and I don't weigh 300 pounds.' But if no one values baseball anymore, the baseball player will be out of business. So I looked into the mirror and said, 'Schlemiel, nobody wants to watch baseball. Make the transformation to football.'" His personal makeover—shedding the role of forgiving father to those widely viewed as not holding their own—helped sway other employees to back a corporate makeover. And his willingness to change helped protect him from attack during the company's long—and generally successful—turnaround period.

Cook the conflict

Managing conflict is one of the greatest challenges a leader of organizational change faces. The conflict may involve resistance to change, or it may involve clashing viewpoints about how the change should be carried out. Often, it will be latent rather than palpable. That's because most organizations are allergic to conflict, seeing it primarily as a source of danger, which it certainly can be. But conflict is a necessary part of the change process and, if handled properly, can serve as the engine of progress.

Thus, a key imperative for a leader trying to achieve significant change is to manage people's passionate differences in a way that diminishes their destructive potential and constructively harnesses their energy. Two techniques can help you achieve this. First, create a secure place where the conflicts can freely bubble up. Second, control the temperature to ensure that the conflict doesn't boil over—and burn you in the process.

The vessel in which a conflict is simmered—in which clashing points of view mix, lose some of their sharpness, and ideally blend into consensus—will look and feel quite different in different contexts. It may be a protected physical space, perhaps an off-site location where an outside facilitator helps a group work through its differences. It may be a clear set of rules and processes that give minority voices confidence that they will be heard without having to disrupt the proceedings to gain attention. It may be the shared language and history of an organization that binds people together through trying times. Whatever its form, it is a place or a means to contain the roiling forces unleashed by the threat of major change.

But a vessel can withstand only so much strain before it blows. A huge challenge you face as a leader is keeping your employees' stress at a productive level. The success of the change effort—as well as your own authority and even survival—requires you to monitor your organization's tolerance for heat and then regulate the temperature accordingly.

You first need to raise the heat enough that people sit up, pay attention, and deal with the real threats and challenges facing them. After all, without some distress, there's no incentive to change. You can constructively raise the temperature by focusing people's attention on the hard issues, by forcing them to take responsibility for tackling and solving those issues, and by bringing conflicts occurring behind closed doors out into the open.

But you have to lower the temperature when necessary to reduce what can be counterproductive turmoil. You can turn down the heat by slowing the pace of change or by tackling some relatively straightforward technical aspect of the problem, thereby reducing people's anxiety levels and allowing them to get warmed up for bigger challenges. You can provide structure to the problem-solving process, creating work groups with specific assignments, setting time parameters, establishing rules for decision-making, and outlining reporting relationships. You can use humor or find an excuse for a break or a party to temporarily ease tensions. You can speak to people's fears and, more critically, to their hopes for a more promising future. By showing people how the future might look, you come to embody hope rather than fear, and you reduce the likelihood of becoming a lightning rod for the conflict.

The aim of both these tactics is to keep the heat high enough to motivate people but low enough to prevent a disastrous explosion—what we call a "productive range of distress." Remember, though, that most employees will reflexively want you to turn down the heat; their complaints may in fact indicate that the environment is just right for hard work to get done.

We've already mentioned a classic example of managing the distress of fundamental change: Franklin Roosevelt during the first few years of his presidency. When he took office in 1933, the chaos, tension, and anxiety brought on by the Depression ran extremely high. Demagogues stoked class, ethnic, and racial conflict that threatened to tear the nation apart. Individuals feared an uncertain future. So Roosevelt first did what he could to reduce the sense of disorder to a tolerable level. He took decisive and authoritative action—he pushed an extraordinary number of bills through Congress during his fabled first 100 days—and thereby gave Americans a sense of direction and safety, reassuring them that they were in capable hands. In his fireside chats, he spoke to people's anxiety and anger and laid out a positive vision for the future that made the stress of the current crisis bearable and seem a worthwhile price to pay for progress.

But he knew the problems facing the nation couldn't be solved from the White House. He needed to mobilize citizens and get them to dream up, try out, fight over, and ultimately own the sometimes painful solutions that would transform the country and move it forward. To do that, he needed to maintain a certain level of fermentation and distress. So, for example, he orchestrated conflicts over public priorities and programs among the large cast of creative people he brought into the government. By giving the same assignment to two different administrators and refusing to clearly define their roles, he got them to generate new and competing ideas. Roosevelt displayed both the acuity to recognize when the tension in the nation had risen too high and the emotional strength to take the heat and permit considerable anxiety to persist.

Place the work where it belongs

Because major change requires people across an entire organization to adapt, you as a leader need to resist the reflex reaction of providing people with the answers. Instead, force yourself to transfer, as Roosevelt did, much of the work and problem-solving to others. If you don't, real and sustainable change won't occur. In addition, it's risky on a personal level to continue to hold on to the work that should be done by others.

As a successful executive, you have gained credibility and authority by demonstrating your capacity to solve other people's problems. This ability can be a virtue, until you find yourself faced with a situation in which you cannot deliver solutions. When this happens, all of your habits, pride, and sense of competence get thrown out of kilter because you must mobilize the work of others rather than find the way yourself. By trying to solve an adaptive challenge for people, at best you will reconfigure it as a technical problem and create some short-term relief. But the issue will not have gone away.

In the 1994 National Basketball Association Eastern Conference semifinals, the Chicago Bulls lost to the New York Knicks in the first two games of the best-of-seven series. Chicago was out to prove that it was more than just a one-man team, that it could win without Michael Jordan, who had retired at the end of the previous season.

In the third game, the score was tied at 102 with less than two seconds left. Chicago had the ball and a time-out to plan a final shot. Coach Phil Jackson called for Scottie Pippen, the Bulls' star since Jordan had retired, to make the inbound pass to Toni Kukoc for the final shot. As play was about to resume, Jackson noticed Pippen sitting at the far end of the bench. Jackson asked him whether he was in or out. "I'm out," said Pippen, miffed that he was not tapped to take the final shot. With only four players on the floor, Jackson quickly called another time-out and substituted an excellent passer, the reserve Pete Myers, for Pippen. Myers tossed a perfect pass to Kukoc, who spun around and sank a miraculous shot to win the game.

The Bulls made their way back to the locker room, their euphoria deflated by Pippen's extraordinary act of insubordination. Jackson recalls that as he entered a silent room, he was uncertain about what to do. Should he punish Pippen? Make him apologize? Pretend the whole thing never happened? All eyes were on him. The coach looked around, meeting the gaze of each player, and said, "What happened has hurt us. Now you have to work this out."

Jackson knew that if he took action to resolve the immediate crisis, he would have made Pippen's behavior a matter between coach and player. But he understood that a deeper issue was at the heart of the incident: Who were the Chicago Bulls without Michael Jordan? It wasn't about who was going to succeed Jordan, because no one was; it was about whether the players could jell as a team where no one person dominated and every player was willing to do whatever it took to help. The issue rested with the players, not him, and only they could resolve it. It did not matter what they decided at that moment; what mattered was that they, not Jackson, did the deciding. What followed was a discussion led by an emotional Bill Cartwright, a team veteran. According to Jackson, the conversation brought the team closer together. The Bulls took the series to a seventh game before succumbing to the Knicks.

Jackson gave the work of addressing both the Pippen and the Jordan issues back to the team for another reason: If he had taken ownership of the problem, he would have become the issue, at least for the moment. In his case, his position as coach probably wouldn't have been threatened. But in other situations, taking responsibility for resolving a conflict within the organization poses risks. You are likely to find yourself resented by the faction that you decide against and held responsible by nearly everyone for the turmoil your decision generates. In the eyes of many, the only way to neutralize the threat is to get rid of you.

Despite that risk, most executives can't resist the temptation to solve fundamental organizational problems by themselves. People expect you to get right in there and fix things, to take a stand and resolve the problem. After all, that is what top managers are paid to do. When you fulfill those expectations, people will call you admirable and courageous—even a "leader"—and that is flattering. But challenging your employees' expectations requires greater courage and leadership.

The Dangers Within

We have described a handful of leadership tactics you can use to interact with the people around you, particularly those who might undermine your initiatives. Those tactics can help advance your initiatives and, just as important, ensure that you remain in a position where you can bring them to fruition. But from our own observations and painful personal experiences, we know that one of the surest ways for an organization to bring you down is simply to let you precipitate your own demise.

In the heat of leadership, with the adrenaline pumping, it is easy to convince yourself that you are not subject to the normal human frailties that can defeat ordinary mortals. You begin to act as if you are indestructible. But the intellectual, physical, and emotional challenges of leadership are fierce. So, in addition to getting on the balcony, you need to regularly step into the inner chamber of your being and assess the tolls those challenges are taking. If you don't, your seemingly indestructible self can self-destruct. This, by the way, is an ideal outcome for your foes—and even friends who oppose your initiative—because no one has to feel responsible for your downfall.

Manage your hungers

We all have hungers, expressions of our normal human needs. But sometimes those hungers disrupt our capacity to act wisely or purposefully. Whether inherited or products of our upbringing, some of these hungers may be so strong that they render us constantly vulnerable. More typically, a stressful situation or setting can exaggerate a normal level of need, amplifying our desires and overwhelming our usual self-discipline. Two of the most common and dangerous hungers are the desire for control and the desire for importance.

Everyone wants to have some measure of control over their life. Yet some people's need for control is disproportionately high. They might have grown up in a household that was either tightly structured or unusually chaotic; in either case, the situation drove them to become masters at taming chaos not only in their own lives but also in their organizations.

That need for control can be a source of vulnerability. Initially, of course, the ability to turn disorder into order may be seen as an attribute. In an organization facing turmoil, you may seem like a godsend if you are able (and desperately want) to step in and take charge. By lowering the distress to a tolerable level, you keep the kettle from boiling over.

But in your desire for order, you can mistake the means for the end. Rather than ensuring that the distress level in an organization remains high enough to mobilize progress on the issues, you focus on maintaining order as an end in itself. Forcing people to make the difficult trade-offs required by fundamental change threatens a return to the disorder you loathe. Your ability to bring the situation under control also suits the people in the organization, who naturally prefer calm to chaos. Unfortunately, this desire for control makes you vulnerable to, and an agent of, the organization's wish to avoid working through contentious issues. While this may ensure your survival in the short term, ultimately you may find yourself accused, justifiably, of failing to deal with the tough challenges when there was still time to do so.

Most people also have some need to feel important and affirmed by others. The danger here is that you will let this affirmation give you an inflated view of yourself and your cause. A grandiose sense of self-importance often leads to self-deception. In particular, you tend to forget the creative role that doubt—which reveals parts of reality that you wouldn't otherwise see—plays in getting your organization to improve. The absence of doubt leads you to see only that which confirms your own competence, which will virtually guarantee disastrous missteps.

Another harmful side effect of an inflated sense of self-importance is that you will encourage people in the organization to become dependent on you. The higher the level of distress, the greater their hopes and expectations that you will provide deliverance. This relieves them of any responsibility for moving the organization forward. But their dependence can be detrimental not only to the group but to you personally. Dependence can quickly turn to contempt as your constituents discover your human shortcomings.

Two well-known stories from the computer industry illustrate the perils of dependency—and how to avoid them. Ken Olsen, the founder of Digital Equipment Corporation, built the company into a 120,000-person operation that, at its peak, was the chief rival of IBM. A generous man, he treated his employees extraordinarily well and experimented with personnel policies designed to increase the creativity, teamwork, and satisfaction of his workforce. This, in tandem with the company's success over the years, led the company's top management to turn to him as the sole decision-maker on all key issues. His decision to shun the personal computer market because of his belief that few people would ever want to own a PC, which seemed reasonable at the time, is generally viewed as the beginning of the end for the company. But that isn't the point; everyone in business makes bad decisions. The point is, Olsen had fostered such an atmosphere of dependence that his decisions were rarely challenged by colleagues—at least not until it was too late.

Contrast that decision with Bill Gates's decision some years later to keep Microsoft out of the internet business. It didn't take long for him to reverse his stand and launch a corporate overhaul that had Microsoft's delivery of internet services as its centerpiece. After watching the rapidly changing computer industry and listening carefully to colleagues, Gates changed his mind with no permanent damage to his sense of pride and an enhanced reputation due to his nimble change of course.

Anchor yourself

To survive the turbulent seas of a change initiative, you need to find ways to steady and stabilize yourself. First, you must establish a safe harbor where each day you can reflect on the previous day's journey, repair the psychological damage you have incurred, renew your stores of emotional resources, and recalibrate your moral compass. Your haven might be a physical place, such as the kitchen table of a friend's house, or a regular routine, such as a daily walk through the neighborhood. Whatever the sanctuary, you need to use and protect it. Unfortunately, seeking such respite is often seen as a luxury, making it one of the first things to go when life gets stressful and you become pressed for time.

Second, you need a confidant, someone you can talk to about what's in your heart and on your mind without fear of being judged or betrayed. Once the undigested mess is on the table, you can begin to separate, with your confidant's honest input, what is worthwhile from what is simply venting. The confidant, typically not a coworker, can also pump you up when you're down and pull you back to earth when you start taking praise too seriously. But don't confuse confidants with allies: Instead of supporting your current initiative, a confidant simply supports you. A common mistake is to seek a confidant among trusted allies, whose personal loyalty may evaporate when a new issue more important to them than you begins to emerge and take center stage.

Perhaps most important, you need to distinguish between your personal self, which can serve as an anchor in stormy weather, and your professional role, which never will. It is easy to mix up the two. And other people only increase the confusion: Colleagues, subordinates, and even bosses often act as if the role you play is the real you. But that is not the case, no matter how much of yourself—your passions, your values, your talents—you genuinely and laudably pour into your professional role. Ask anyone who has experienced the rude awakening that comes when they leave a position of authority and suddenly find that their phone calls aren't returned as quickly as they used to be.

That harsh lesson holds another important truth that is easily forgotten: When people attack someone in a position of authority, more often than not they are attacking the role, not the person. Even when attacks on you are highly personal, you need to read them primarily as reactions to how you, in your role, are affecting people's lives. Understanding the criticism for what it is prevents it from undermining your stability and sense of self-worth. And that's important because when you feel the sting of an attack, you are likely to become defensive and lash out at your critics, which can precipitate your downfall.

We hasten to add that criticism may contain legitimate points about how you are performing your role. For example, you may have been tactless in raising an issue with your organization, or you may have turned the heat up too quickly on a change initiative. But, at its heart, the criticism is usually about the issue, not you. Through the guise of attacking you personally, people often are simply trying to neutralize the threat they perceive in your point of view. Does anyone ever attack you when you hand out big checks or deliver good news? People attack your personality, style, or judgment when they don't like the message.

When you take "personal" attacks personally, you unwittingly conspire in one of the common ways you can be taken out of action—you make yourself the issue. Contrast the manner in which presidential candidates Gary Hart and Bill Clinton handled charges of philandering. Hart angrily counterattacked, criticizing the scruples of the reporters who had shadowed him. This defensive personal response kept the focus on his behavior. Clinton, on national television, essentially admitted he had strayed, acknowledging his piece of the mess. His strategic handling of the situation allowed him to return the campaign's focus to policy issues. Though both attacks were extremely personal, only Clinton understood that they were basically attacks on positions he represented and the role he was seeking to play.

Do not underestimate the difficulty of distinguishing self from role and responding coolly to what feels like a personal attack—particularly when the criticism comes, as it will, from people you care about. But disciplining yourself to do so can provide you with an anchor that will keep you from running aground and give you the stability to remain calm, focused, and persistent in engaging people with the tough issues.

Why Lead?

We will have failed if this "survival manual" for avoiding the perils of leadership causes you to become cynical or callous in your leadership effort or to shun the challenges of leadership altogether. We haven't touched on the thrill of inspiring people to come up with creative solutions that can transform an organization for the better. We hope we have shown that the essence of leadership lies in the capacity to deliver disturbing news and raise difficult questions in a way that moves people to take up the message rather than kill the messenger. But we haven't talked about the reasons that someone might want to take these risks.

Of course, many people who strive for high-authority positions are attracted to power. But in the end, that isn't enough to make the high stakes of the game worthwhile. We would argue that, when they look deep within themselves, people grapple with the challenges of leadership in order to make a positive difference in the lives of others.

When corporate presidents and vice presidents reach their late fifties, they often look back on careers devoted to winning in the marketplace. They may have succeeded remarkably, yet some people have difficulty making sense of their lives in light of what they have given up. For too many, their accomplishments seem empty. They question whether they should have been more aggressive in questioning corporate purposes or creating more ambitious visions for their companies.

Our underlying assumption in this article is that you can lead *and* stay alive—not just register a pulse but really be alive. But the classic protective devices of a person in authority tend to insulate them from those qualities that foster an acute experience of living. Cynicism, often dressed up as realism, undermines creativity and daring. Arrogance, often posing as authoritative knowledge, snuffs out curiosity and the eagerness to question. Callousness, sometimes portrayed as the thick skin of experience, shuts out compassion for others.

The hard truth is that it is not possible to know the rewards and joys of leadership without experiencing the pain as well. But staying in the game and bearing that pain is worth it, not only for the positive changes you can make in the lives of others but also for the meaning it gives your own.

Originally published in June 2002. Reprint R0206C

9

The Real Reason People Won't Change

by Robert Kegan and Lisa Lahey

Every manager is familiar with the employee who just won't change. Sometimes it's easy to see why—the employee fears a shift in power, the need to learn new skills, the stress of having to join a new team. In other cases, such resistance is far more puzzling. An employee has the skills and smarts to make a change with ease, has shown a deep commitment to the company, genuinely supports the change—and yet, inexplicably, does nothing.

What's going on? As organizational psychologists, we have seen this dynamic literally hundreds of times, and our research and analysis have recently led us to a surprising yet deceptively simple conclusion. Resistance to change does not reflect opposition, nor is it merely a result of inertia. Instead, even as they hold a sincere commitment to change, many people are unwittingly applying productive energy toward a hidden *competing commitment*. The resulting dynamic equilibrium stalls the effort in what looks like resistance but is in fact a kind of personal immunity to change.

When you, as a manager, uncover an employee's competing commitment, behavior that has seemed irrational and ineffective suddenly becomes stunningly sensible and masterful—but unfortunately, on behalf of a goal that conflicts with what you and even the employee are trying to achieve. You find out that the project leader who's dragging his feet has an unrecognized competing commitment to avoid the even tougher assignment—one he fears he can't handle—that might come his way next if he delivers too successfully on the task at hand. Or you find that the person who won't collaborate despite a passionate and sincere commitment to teamwork is equally dedicated to avoiding the conflict that naturally attends any ambitious team activity.

In these pages, we'll look at competing commitments in detail and take you through a process to help your employees overcome their immunity to change. The process may sound straightforward, but it is by no means quick or easy. On the contrary, it challenges the very psychological foundations upon which people function. It asks people to call into question beliefs they've long held close, perhaps since childhood. And it requires people to admit to painful, even embarrassing, feelings that they would not ordinarily disclose to others or even to themselves. Indeed, some people will opt not to disrupt their immunity to change, choosing instead to continue their fruitless struggle against their competing commitments.

As a manager, you must guide people through this exercise with understanding and sensitivity. If your employees are to engage in honest introspection and candid disclosure, they must understand that their revelations won't be used against them. The goal of this exploration is solely to help them become more

Idea in Brief

Tearing out your managerial hair over employees who just won't change—especially the ones who are clearly smart, skilled, and deeply committed to your company and your plans for improvement?

Before you throw up your hands in frustration, listen to recent psychological research: These otherwise valued employees aren't purposefully subversive or resistant. Instead, they may be unwittingly caught in a competing commitment—a subconscious, hidden goal that conflicts with their stated commitments. For example: A project leader dragging his feet has an unrecognized competing commitment to avoid tougher assignments that may come his way if he delivers too successfully on the current project.

Competing commitments make people personally immune to change. Worse, they can undermine your best employees'—and your company's—success.

If the thought of tackling these hidden commitments strikes you as a psychological quagmire, you're not alone. However, you can help employees uncover and move beyond their competing commitments—without having to "put them on the couch." But take care: You'll be challenging employees' deepest psychological foundations and questioning their longest-held beliefs.

Why bother, you ask? Consider the rewards: You help talented employees become much more effective and make far more significant contributions to your company. And, you discover what's really going on when people who seem genuinely committed to change dig in their heels.

effective, not to find flaws in their work or character. As you support your employees in unearthing and challenging their innermost assumptions, you may at times feel you're playing the role of a psychologist. But in a sense, managers *are* psychologists. After all, helping people overcome their limitations to become more successful at work is at the very heart of effective management.

We'll describe this delicate process in detail, but first let's look at some examples of competing commitments in action.

Shoveling Sand Against the Tide

Competing commitments cause valued employees to behave in ways that seem inexplicable and irremediable, and this is enormously frustrating to managers. Take the case of John, a talented manager at a software company. (Like all examples in this article, John's experiences are real, although we have altered identifying features. In some cases, we've constructed composite examples.) John was a big believer in open communication and valued close working relationships, yet his caustic sense of humor consistently kept colleagues at a distance. And though he wanted to move up in the organization, his personal style was holding him back. Repeatedly, John was counseled on his behavior, and he readily agreed that he needed to change the way he interacted with others in the organization. But time after time, he reverted to his old patterns. Why, his boss wondered, did John continue to undermine his own advancement?

As it happened, John was a person of color working as part of an otherwise all-white executive team. When he went through an exercise designed to help him unearth his competing commitments, he made a surprising discovery about himself. Underneath it all, John believed that if he became too well integrated with the team, it would threaten his sense of loyalty to his own racial group. Moving too close to the mainstream made him feel very uncomfortable, as if he were becoming "one of them" and betraying his family and friends. So when people gathered around his ideas and suggestions, he'd tear down their support with sarcasm, inevitably (and effectively) returning himself to the margins, where he was more at ease. In short, while John was genuinely committed to working well with his colleagues, he had an equally powerful competing commitment to keeping his distance.

Consider, too, a manager we'll call Helen, a rising star at a large manufacturing company. Helen had been assigned responsibility for speeding up production of the company's most popular product, yet she was spinning her wheels. When her boss, Andrew, realized that an important deadline was only two months away and she hadn't filed a single progress report, he called her into a meeting to discuss the project. Helen agreed that she was far behind schedule, acknowledging that she had been stalling in pulling together the team. But at the same time, she showed a genuine commitment to making the project a success. The two developed a detailed plan for changing direction, and Andrew assumed the problem was resolved. But three weeks after the meeting, Helen still hadn't launched the team.

Why was Helen unable to change her behavior? After intense self-examination in a workshop with several of her colleagues, she came to an unexpected conclusion: Although she truly wanted the project to succeed, she had an accompanying, unacknowledged commitment to maintaining a subordinate position in relation to Andrew. At a deep level, Helen was concerned that if she succeeded in her new role—one she was excited about and eager to undertake—she would become more a peer than a subordinate. She was uncertain whether Andrew was prepared for the turn their relationship would take. Worse, a promotion would mean that she, not Andrew, would be ultimately accountable for the results of her work—and Helen feared she wouldn't be up to the task.

These stories shed some light on the nature of immunity to change. The inconsistencies between John's and Helen's stated goals and their actions reflect neither hypocrisy nor unspoken reluctance to change but the paralyzing effect of competing commitments. Any manager who seeks to help John communicate more effectively or Helen move her project forward, without understanding that each is also struggling unconsciously toward an opposing agenda, is shoveling sand against the tide.

Diagnosing Immunity to Change

Competing commitments aren't distressing only to the boss; they're frustrating to employees as well. People with the most sincere intentions often unwittingly create for themselves Sisyphean tasks. And they are almost always tremendously relieved when they discover just *why* they feel as if they are rolling a boulder up a hill only to have it roll back down again. Even though uncovering a competing commitment can open up a host of new concerns, the discovery offers hope for finally accomplishing the primary, stated commitment.

Based on the past 15 years of working with hundreds of managers in a variety of companies, we've developed a three-stage process to help organizations figure out what's getting in the way of change. First, managers guide employees through a set of questions designed to uncover competing commitments. Next, employees examine these commitments to determine the underlying assumptions at their core. And finally, employees start the process of changing their behavior.

We'll walk through the process fairly quickly below, but it's important to note that each step will take time. Just uncovering the competing commitment will require at least two or three hours, because people need to reflect on each question and the implications of their answers. The process of challenging competing commitments and making real progress toward overcoming immunity to change unfolds over a longer period—weeks or even months. But just getting the commitments on the table can

Getting Groups to Change

Although competing commitments and big assumptions tend to be deeply personal, groups are just as susceptible as individuals to the dynamics of immunity to change. Face-to-face teams, departments, and even companies as a whole can fall prey to inner contradictions that "protect" them from significant changes they may genuinely strive for. The leadership team of a video production company, for instance, enjoyed a highly collaborative, largely flat organizational structure. A year before we met the group, team members had undertaken a planning process that led them to a commitment of which they were unanimously in favor: In order to ensure that the company would grow in the way the team wished, each of the principals would take responsibility for aggressively overseeing a distinct market segment.

The members of the leadership team told us they came out of this process with a great deal of momentum. They knew which markets to target, they had formed some concrete plans for moving forward, and they had clearly assigned accountability for each market. Yet a year later, the group had to admit it had accomplished very little, despite the enthusiasm. There were lots of rational explanations: "We were unrealistic; we thought we could do new things and still have time to keep meeting our present obligations." "We didn't pursue new clients aggressively enough." "We tried new things but gave up too quickly if they didn't immediately pay off."

Efforts to overcome these barriers—to pursue clients more aggressively, for instance—didn't work because they didn't get to the cause of the unproductive behavior. But by seeing the team's explanations as a potential window into the bigger competing commitment, we were able to help the group better understand its predicament. We asked, "Can you identify even the vaguest fear or worry about what might happen if you *did* more aggressively pursue the new markets? Or if you reduced some of your present activity on behalf of building the new business?" Before long, a different discourse began to emerge, and the other half of a striking groupwide contradiction came into view: The principals were worried that pursuing the plan would drive them apart functionally and emotionally.

(continued)

> **Getting Groups to Change** (*continued*)
>
> "We now realize we are also committed to preserving the noncompetitive, intellectually rewarding, and cocreative spirit of our corporate enterprise," they concluded. On behalf of this commitment, the team members had to commend themselves on how "noncompetitively" and "cocreatively" they were finding ways to undermine the strategic plans they still believed were the best route to the company's future success. The team's big assumptions? "We assumed that pursuing the target-market strategy, with each of us taking aggressive responsibility for a given segment, would create the 'silos' we have long happily avoided and would leave us more isolated from one another. We also assumed the strategy would make us more competitively disposed toward one another." Whether or not the assumptions were true, they would have continued to block the group's efforts until they were brought to light. In fact, as the group came to discover, there were a variety of moves that would allow the leadership team to preserve a genuinely collaborative collegiality while pursuing the new corporate strategy.

have a noticeable effect on the decisions people make and the actions they take.

Uncovering Competing Commitments

Overcoming immunity to change starts with uncovering competing commitments. In our work, we've found that even though people keep their competing commitments well hidden, you can draw them out by asking a series of questions—as long as the employees believe that personal and potentially embarrassing disclosures won't be used inappropriately. It can be very powerful to guide people through this diagnostic exercise in a group—typically with several volunteers making their own discoveries public—so people can see that others, even the company's star performers, have competing commitments and inner contradictions of their own.

The first question we ask is, *What would you like to see changed at work, so that you could be more effective or so that work would be more satisfying?* Responses to this question are nearly always couched in a complaint—a form of communication that most managers bemoan because of its negative, unproductive tone. But complaints can be immensely useful. People complain only about the things they care about, and they complain the loudest about the things they care about most. With little effort, people can turn their familiar, uninspiring gripes into something that's more likely to energize and motivate them—a commitment, genuinely their own.

To get there, you need to ask a second question: *What commitments does your complaint imply?* A project leader we worked with, we'll call him Tom, had grumbled, "My subordinates keep me out of the loop on important developments in my project." This complaint yielded the statement, "I believe in open and candid communication." A line manager we'll call Mary lamented people's unwillingness to speak up at meetings; her complaint implied a commitment to shared decision-making.

While undoubtedly sincere in voicing such commitments, people can nearly always identify some way in which they are in part responsible for preventing them from being fulfilled. Thus, the third question is: *What are* you *doing, or not doing, that is keeping your commitment from being more fully realized?* Invariably, in our experience, people can identify these undermining behaviors in just a couple of seconds. For example, Tom admitted: "When people bring me bad news, I tend to shoot the messenger." And Mary acknowledged that she didn't delegate much

A diagnostic test for immunity to change

The most important steps in diagnosing immunity to change are uncovering employees' competing commitments and unearthing their big assumptions. To do so, we ask a series of questions and record key responses in a simple grid. Below we've listed the responses for six people who went through this exercise, including the examples described in the text. The grid paints a picture of the change-immunity system, making sense of a previously puzzling dynamic.

	Stated commitment I am committed to...	What am I doing, or not doing, that is keeping my stated commitment from being fully realized?	Competing commitments	Big assumptions
John	...high-quality communication with my colleagues.	Sometimes I use sarcastic humor to get my point across.	I am committed to maintaining a distance from my white colleagues.	I assume I will lose my authentic connection to my racial group if I get too integrated into the mainstream.
Helen	...the new initiative.	I don't push for top performance from my team members or myself; I accept mediocre products and thinking too often; I don't prioritize.	I am committed to not upsetting my relationship with my boss by leaving the mentee role.	I assume my boss will stop supporting me if I move toward becoming his peer; I assume that I don't have what it takes to successfully carry out a cutting-edge project.
Tom	...hearing from my subordinates and maximizing the flow of information into my office.	I don't ask questions or ask to be kept in the loop on sensitive or delicate matters; I shoot the messenger when I hear bad news.	I am committed to not learning about things I can't do anything about.	I assume that as a leader I should be able to address all problems; I assume I will be seen as incompetent if I can't solve all problems that come up.

Mary	...distributed leadership by enabling people to make decisions.	I don't delegate enough; I don't pass on the necessary information to the people I distribute leadership to.	I am committed to having things go my way, to being in control, and to ensuring that the work is done to my high standards.	I assume that other people will waste my time and theirs if I don't step in; I assume others aren't as smart as I am.
Bill	...being a team player.	I don't collaborate enough; I make unilateral decisions too often; I don't really take people's input into account.	I am committed to being the one who gets the credit and to avoiding the frustration or conflict that comes with collaboration.	I assume that no one will appreciate me if I am not seen as the source of success; I assume nothing good will come of my being frustrated or in conflict.
Jane	...turning around my department.	Too often I let things slide; I'm not proactive enough in getting people to follow through with their tasks.	I am committed to not setting full sail until I have a clear map of how we get our department from here to there.	I assume that if I take my group out into deep waters and discover I am unable to get us to the other side, I will be seen as an incompetent leader who is undeserving of trust or responsibility.

and that she sometimes didn't release all the information people needed in order to make good decisions.

In both cases, there may well have been other circumstances contributing to the shortfalls, but clearly both Tom and Mary were engaging in behavior that was affecting the people around them. Most people recognize this about themselves right away and are quick to say, "I need to stop doing that." Indeed, Tom had repeatedly vowed to listen more openly to potential problems that would slow his projects. However, the purpose of this exercise is not to make these behaviors disappear—at least not now. The purpose is to understand why people behave in ways that undermine their own success.

The next step, then, is to invite people to consider the consequences of forgoing the behavior. We do this by asking a fourth question: *If you imagine doing the opposite of the undermining behavior, do you detect in yourself any discomfort, worry, or vague fear?* Tom imagined himself listening calmly and openly to some bad news about a project and concluded, "I'm afraid I'll hear about a problem that I can't fix, something that I can't do anything about." And Mary? She considered allowing people more latitude and realized that, quite frankly, she feared people wouldn't make good decisions and she would be forced to carry out a strategy she thought would lead to an inferior result.

The final step is to transform that passive fear into a statement that reflects an active commitment to preventing certain outcomes. We ask, *By engaging in this undermining behavior, what worrisome outcome are you committed to preventing?* The resulting answer is the competing commitment, which lies at the very heart of a person's immunity to change. Tom admitted, "I am committed to not learning about problems I can't fix." By intimidating his staff, he prevented them from delivering bad news, protecting himself from the fear that he was not in control of the project. Mary, too, was protecting herself—in her case, against the consequences of bad decisions. "I am committed to making sure my group does not make decisions that I don't like."

Such revelations can feel embarrassing. While primary commitments nearly always reflect noble goals that people would be happy to shout from the rooftops, competing commitments are very personal, reflecting vulnerabilities that people fear will undermine how they are regarded both by others and themselves. Little wonder people keep them hidden and hasten to cover them up again once they're on the table.

But competing commitments should not be seen as weaknesses. They represent some version of self-protection, a perfectly natural and reasonable human impulse. The question is, if competing commitments are a form of self-protection, what are people protecting themselves from? The answers usually lie in what we call their *big assumptions*—deeply rooted beliefs about themselves and the world around them. These assumptions put an order to the world and at the same time suggest ways in which the world can go out of order. Competing commitments arise from these assumptions, driving behaviors unwittingly designed to keep the picture intact.

Examining the Big Assumption

People rarely realize they hold big assumptions because, quite simply, they accept them as reality. Often formed long ago and seldom, if ever, critically examined, big assumptions are woven into the very fabric of people's existence. (For more on the grip

> ## Big Assumptions: How Our Perceptions Shape Our Reality
>
> Big assumptions reflect the very human manner in which we invent or shape a picture of the world and then take our inventions for reality. This is easiest to see in children. The delight we take in their charming distortions is a kind of celebration that they are actively making sense of the world, even if a bit eccentrically. As one story goes, two youngsters had been learning about Hindu culture and were taken with a representation of the universe in which the world sits atop a giant elephant, and the elephant sits atop an even more giant turtle. "I wonder what the turtle sits on," says one of the children. "I think from then on," says the other, "it's turtles all the way down."
>
> But deep within our amusement may lurk a note of condescension, an implication that this is what distinguishes children from grown-ups. Their meaning-making is subject to youthful distortions, we assume. Ours represents an accurate map of reality.
>
> But does it? Are we really finished discovering, once we have reached adulthood, that our maps don't match the territory? The answer is clearly no. In our 20 years of longitudinal and cross-sectional

that big assumptions hold on people, see the sidebar "Big Assumptions: How Our Perceptions Shape Our Reality.") But with a little help, most people can call them up fairly easily, especially once they've identified their competing commitments. To do this, we first ask people to create the beginning of a sentence by inverting the competing commitment, and then we ask them to fill in the blank. For Tom ("I am committed to not hearing about problems I can't fix"), the big assumption turned out to be, "I assume that if I *did* hear about problems I can't fix, people would discover I'm not qualified to do my job." Mary's big assumption was that her teammates weren't as smart or experienced as

> research, we've discovered that adults must grow into and out of several qualitatively different views of the world if they are to master the challenges of their life experiences (see Robert Kegan, *In Over Our Heads,* Harvard University Press, 1994).
>
> A woman we met from Australia told us about her experience living in the United States for a year. "Not only do you drive on the wrong side of the street over here," she said, "your steering wheels are on the wrong side, too. I would routinely pile into the right side of the car to drive off, only to discover I needed to get out and walk over to the other side.
>
> "One day," she continued, "I was thinking about six different things, and I got into the right side of the car, took out my keys, and was prepared to drive off. I looked up and thought to myself, 'My God, here in the violent and lawless United States, they are even stealing *steering wheels!*'"
>
> Of course, the countervailing evidence was just an arm's length to her left, but—and this is the main point—*why should she look?* Our big assumptions create a disarming and deluding sense of certainty. If we know where a steering wheel belongs, we are unlikely to look for it someplace else. If we know what our company, department, boss, or subordinate can and can't do, why should we look for countervailing data—even if it is just an arm's length away?

she and that she'd be wasting her time and others' if she didn't maintain control. Returning to our earlier story, John's big assumption might be, "I assume that if I develop unambivalent relationships with my white coworkers, I will sacrifice my racial identity and alienate my own community."

This is a difficult process, and it doesn't happen all at once, because admitting to big assumptions makes people uncomfortable. The process can put names to very personal feelings people are reluctant to disclose, such as deep-seated fears or insecurities, highly discouraging or simplistic views of human nature, or perceptions of their own superior abilities or intellect.

Unquestioning acceptance of a big assumption anchors and sustains an immune system: A competing commitment makes all the sense in the world, and the person continues to engage in behaviors that support it, albeit unconsciously, to the detriment of their "official," stated commitment. Only by bringing big assumptions to light can people finally challenge their assumptions and recognize why they are engaging in seemingly contradictory behavior.

Questioning the Big Assumption

Once people have identified their competing commitments and the big assumptions that sustain them, most are prepared to take some immediate action to overcome their immunity. But the first part of the process involves observation, not action, which can be frustrating for high achievers accustomed to leaping into motion to solve problems. Let's take a look at the steps in more detail.

Step 1: Notice and record current behavior

Employees must first take notice of what does and doesn't happen as a consequence of holding big assumptions to be true. We specifically ask people *not* to try to make any changes in their thinking or behavior at this time but just to become more aware of their actions in relation to their big assumptions. This gives people the opportunity to develop a better appreciation for how and in what contexts big assumptions influence their lives. John, for example, who had assumed that working well with his white colleagues would estrange him from his ethnic group, saw that he had missed an opportunity to get involved in an exciting, high-profile initiative because he had mocked the idea when it first came up in a meeting.

Step 2: Look for contrary evidence

Next, employees must look actively for experiences that might cast doubt on the validity of their big assumptions. Because big assumptions are held as fact, they actually inform what people see, leading them to systematically (but unconsciously) attend to certain data and avoid or ignore other data. By asking people to search specifically for experiences that would cause them to question their assumptions, we help them see that they have been filtering out certain types of information—information that could weaken the grip of the big assumptions.

When John looked around him, he considered for the first time that an African American manager in another department had strong working relationships with her mostly white colleagues yet seemed not to have compromised her personal identity. He also had to admit that when he had been thrown onto an urgent task force the year before, he had worked many hours alongside his white colleagues and found the experience satisfying; he had felt none of his usual ambivalence.

Step 3: Explore the history

In this step, we ask people to become the "biographers" of their assumptions: How and when did the assumptions first take hold? How long have they been around? What have been some of their critical turning points?

Typically, this step leads people to earlier life experiences, almost always to times before their current jobs and relationships with current coworkers. This reflection usually makes people dissatisfied with the foundations of their big assumptions, especially when they see that these have accompanied them to their current positions and have been coloring their experiences for many years. Recently, a CEO expressed astonishment as she realized she'd been applying the same self-protective stance in her work that she'd developed during a difficult divorce years before. Just as commonly, as was the case for John, people trace their big assumptions to early experiences with parents, siblings, or friends. Understanding the circumstances that influenced the formation of the assumptions can free people to consider whether these beliefs apply to their present selves.

Step 4: Test the assumption

This step entails creating and running a modest test of the big assumption. This is the first time we ask people to consider making changes in their behavior. Each employee should come up with a scenario and run it by a partner who serves as a sounding board. (Left to their own devices, people tend to create tests that are either too risky or so tentative that they don't actually challenge the assumption and in fact reaffirm its validity.) After conferring with a partner, John, for instance, volunteered to join a short-term committee looking at his department's process for evaluating new product ideas. Because the team would dissolve after a month, he would be able to extricate himself fairly quickly if he grew too uncomfortable with the relationships. But the experience would force him to spend a significant amount of time with several of his white colleagues during that month and would provide him an opportunity to test his sense of the real costs of being a full team member.

Step 5: Evaluate the results

In the last step, employees evaluate the test results, evaluate the test itself, design and run new tests, and eventually question the big assumptions. For John, this meant signing up for other initiatives and making initial social overtures to white coworkers. At the same time, by engaging in volunteer efforts within his community outside of work, he made sure that his ties to his racial group were not compromised.

It is worth noting that revealing a big assumption doesn't necessarily mean it will be exposed as false. But even if a big assumption does contain an element of truth, an individual can often find more effective ways to operate once they have had a chance to challenge the assumption and its hold on their behavior. Indeed, John found a way to support the essence of his competing commitment—to maintain his bond with his racial group—while minimizing behavior that sabotaged his other stated commitments.

Uncovering Your Own Immunity

As you go through this process with your employees, remember that managers are every bit as susceptible to change immunity as employees are, and your competing commitments and big assumptions can have a significant impact on the people around you. Returning once more to Helen's story: When we went through this exercise with her boss, Andrew, it turned out that he was harboring some contradictions of his own. While he was committed to the success of his subordinates, Andrew at some level assumed that he alone could meet his high standards, and as a result he was laboring under a competing commitment to maintain absolute control over his projects. He was unintentionally communicating this lack of confidence to his subordinates—including Helen—in subtle ways. In the end, Andrew's and Helen's competing commitments were, without their knowledge, mutually reinforcing, keeping Helen dependent on Andrew and allowing Andrew to control her projects.

Helen and Andrew are still working through this process, but they've already gained invaluable insight into their behavior and the ways they are impeding their own progress. This may seem like a small step, but bringing these issues to the surface and confronting them head-on is challenging and painful—yet tremendously effective. It allows managers to see, at last, what's really going on when people who are genuinely committed to change nonetheless dig in their heels. It's not about identifying unproductive behavior and systematically making plans to correct it, as if treating symptoms would cure a disease. It's not about coaxing or cajoling or even giving poor performance reviews. It's about understanding the complexities of people's behavior, guiding them through a productive process to bring their competing commitments to the surface, and helping them cope with the inner conflict that is preventing them from achieving their goals.

Originally published in November 2001. Reprint R0110E

10

Your Workforce Is More Adaptable Than You Think

by Joseph Fuller, Judith K. Wallenstein, Manjari Raman, and Alice de Chalendar

Many managers have little faith in their employees' ability to survive the twists and turns of a rapidly evolving economy. "The majority of people in disappearing jobs do not realize what is coming," the head of strategy at a top German bank recently told us. "My call center workers are neither able nor willing to change."

This kind of thinking is common, but it's wrong, as we learned after surveying thousands of employees around the world. In 2018, in an attempt to understand the various forces shaping the nature of work, Harvard Business School's Project on Managing the Future of Work and the Boston Consulting Group's Henderson Institute came together to conduct a survey spanning 11 countries—Brazil, China, France, Germany, India, Indonesia,

Japan, Spain, Sweden, the United Kingdom, and the United States—gathering responses from 1,000 workers in each. In it we focused solely on the people most vulnerable to changing dynamics: lower-income and middle-skills workers. The majority of them were earning less than the average household income in their countries, and all of them had no more than two years of postsecondary education. In each of eight countries—Brazil, China, France, Germany, India, Japan, the United Kingdom, and the United States—we then surveyed at least 800 business leaders (whose companies differed from those of the workers we surveyed). In total we gathered responses from 11,000 workers and 6,500 business leaders.

What we learned was fascinating: The two groups perceived the future in significantly different ways. Given the complexity of the changes that companies are confronting today and the speed with which they need to make decisions, this gap in perceptions has serious and far-reaching consequences for managers and employees alike.

Predictably, business leaders feel anxious as they struggle to marshal and mobilize the workforce of tomorrow. In a climate of perpetual disruption, how can they find and hire employees who have the skills their companies need? And what should they do with people whose skills have become obsolete? The CEO of one multinational company told us he was so tormented by that last question that he had to seek counsel from his priest.

The workers, however, didn't share that sense of anxiety. Instead, they focused more on the opportunities and benefits that the future holds for them, and they revealed themselves to be much more eager to embrace change and learn new skills than their employers gave them credit for.

Idea in Brief

The Problem
As they try to build a workforce in a climate of perpetual disruption, business leaders worry that their employees can't—or just won't—adapt to the big changes that lie ahead. How can companies find people with the skills they will need?

What the Research Shows
Harvard Business School and the BCG Henderson Institute surveyed thousands of business leaders and workers around the world and discovered an important gap in perceptions: Workers are far more willing and able to embrace change than their employers assume.

The Solution
This gap represents an opportunity. Companies need to start thinking of their employees as a reserve of talent and energy that can be tapped by providing smart on-the-job skills training and career development.

The Nature of the Gap

When executives today consider the forces that are changing how work is done, they tend to think mostly about disruptive *technologies*. But that's too narrow a focus. A remarkably broad set of forces is transforming the nature of work, and companies need to take them all into account.

In our research we've identified 17 forces of disruption, which we group into six basic categories. Our surveys explored the attitudes that business leaders and workers had toward each of them. In their responses, we were able to discern three notable differences in the ways that the two groups think about the future of work.

The first is that *workers seem to recognize more clearly than leaders do that their organizations are contending with multiple*

The Forces Shaping the Future of Work

Accelerating Technological Change

- New technologies that replace human labor, threatening employment (such as driverless trucks)
- New technologies that augment or supplement human labor (for example, robots in health care)
- Sudden technology-based shifts in customer needs that result in new business models, new ways of working, or faster product innovation
- Technology-enabled opportunities to monetize free services (such as Amazon Web Services) or underutilized assets (such as personal consumption data)

Growing Demand for Skills

- General increase in the skills, technical knowledge, and formal education required to perform work
- Growing shortage of workers with the skills for rapidly evolving jobs

Changing Employee Expectations

- Increased popularity of flexible, self-directed forms of work that allow better work-life balance
- More widespread desire for work with a purpose and opportunities to influence the way it is delivered (for example, greater team autonomy)

Shifting Labor Demographics

- Need to increase workforce participation of underrepresented populations (such as elderly workers, women, immigrants, and rural workers)

Transitioning Work Models

- Rise of remote work
- Growth of contingent forms of work (such as on-call workers, temp workers, and contractors)
- Freelancing and labor-sharing platforms that provide access to talent
- Delivery of work through complex partner ecosystems (involving multiple industries, geographies, and organizations of different sizes), rather than within a single organization

Evolving Business Environment

- New regulation aimed at controlling technology use (for example, "robot taxes")
- Regulatory changes that affect wage levels, either directly (such as minimum wages or Social Security entitlements) or indirectly (such as more public income assistance or universal basic income)
- Regulatory shifts affecting cross-border flow of goods, services, and capital
- Greater economic and political volatility as members of society feel left behind

forces of disruption, each of which will affect how companies work differently. When asked to rate the impact that each of the 17 forces would have on their work lives, using a 100-point scale, the employees rated the force with the strongest impact 15 points higher than the force with the weakest impact. In comparison, there was only a 9-point spread between the forces rated the strongest and the weakest by managers.

In fact, the leaders seemed unable or unwilling to think in differentiated ways about the forces' potential for disruption. When asked about each force, roughly a third of them described it as having a significant impact on their organization today; close to half projected that it would have a significant impact in the future; and about a fifth claimed it would have no impact at all. That's a troubling level of uniformity, and it suggests that most leaders haven't yet figured out which forces of change they should make a priority.

Interestingly, workers appeared to be more aware of the opportunities and challenges of several of the forces. Notably, workers focused on the growing importance of the gig economy, and they ranked "freelancing and labor-sharing platforms" as the third most significant of all 17 forces. Business leaders, however, ranked that force as the least significant.

The second difference that emerged from our survey was this: *Workers seem to be more adaptive and optimistic about the future than their leaders recognize.*

The conventional wisdom, of course, is that workers fear that technology will make their jobs obsolete. But our survey revealed that to be a misconception. A majority of the workers felt that advances such as automation and artificial intelligence would have a positive impact on their future. In fact, they felt that way about two-thirds of the forces. What concerned them most were the forces that might allow *other workers*—temporary, freelance, outsourced—to take their jobs.

When asked why they had a positive outlook, workers most commonly cited two reasons: the prospect of better wages and the prospect of more interesting and meaningful jobs. Both automation and technology, they felt, heralded opportunity on those fronts—by contributing to the emergence of more-flexible and self-directed forms of work, by creating alternative ways to earn income, and by making it possible to avoid tasks that were "dirty, dangerous, or dull."

In every country, workers described themselves as more willing to prepare for the workplace of the future than managers believed them to be (in Japan, though, the percentages were nearly equal). Yet when asked what was holding workers back, managers chose answers that blamed employees, rather than themselves. Their most common response was that workers feared significant change. The idea that workers might lack the support they needed from employers was only their fifth-most-popular response.

That brings us to our third finding: *Workers are seeking more support and guidance to prepare themselves for future employment than management is providing.*

In every country except France and Japan, significant majorities of workers reported that they—and not their government or their employer—were responsible for equipping themselves to meet the needs of a rapidly evolving workplace. That held true across age groups and for both men and women. But workers also felt that they had serious obstacles to overcome: a lack of knowledge about their options; a lack of time to prepare for the future; high training costs; the impact that taking time off for training would have on wages; and, in particular, insufficient support from their employers. All are barriers that management can and should help workers get past.

What Employers Can Do to Help

The gap in perspectives is a problem because it leads managers to underestimate employees' ambitions and underinvest in their skills. But it also shows that there's a vast reserve of talent and energy companies can tap into to ready themselves for the future: their workers.

The challenge is figuring out how best to do that. We've identified five important ways to get started.

1. Don't just set up training programs—create a learning culture

If companies today engage in training, they tend to do it at specific times (when onboarding new hires, for example), to prepare workers for particular jobs (like selling and servicing certain products), or when adopting new technologies. That worked well in an era when the pace of technological change was relatively slow. But advances are happening so quickly and with such complexity today that companies need to shift to a continuous-learning model—one that repeatedly enhances employees' skills and makes formal training broadly available. Firms also need to expand their portfolio of tactics beyond online and offline courses to include learning on the job through project staffing and team rotations. Such an approach can help companies rethink traditional entry-level barriers (among them, educational credentials) and draw from a wider talent pool.

Consider what happens at Expeditors, a *Fortune* 500 company that provides global logistics and freight-forwarding services in more than 100 countries. In vetting job candidates, Expeditors has long relied on a "hire for attitude, train for skill" approach. Educational degrees are appreciated but not seen as critical for success in most roles. Instead, for all positions, from the lowest level right up to the C-suite, the company focuses on temperament and cultural fit. Once on staff, employees join an intensive program in which every member of the organization, no matter how junior or senior, undertakes 52 hours of incremental learning a year. This practice supports the company's promote-from-within culture. Expeditors' efforts seem to be working: Turnover is low (which means substantial savings in hiring, training, and onboarding costs); retention is high (a third of the company's 17,000 employees have worked at the company for 10 years or more); most senior leaders in the company have risen through the ranks; and several current vice presidents and senior vice presidents, along with the current and former CEOs, got their jobs despite having no college degree.

2. Engage employees in the transition instead of herding them through it

As companies transform themselves, they often find it a challenge to attract and retain the type of talent they need. To succeed, they have to offer employees pathways to professional and personal improvement—and must engage them in the process of change, rather than merely inform them that change is coming.

That's what ING Netherlands did in 2014, when it decided to reinvent itself. The bank's goal was ambitious: to turn itself into an agile institution almost overnight. The company's current CEO, Vincent van den Boogert, recalls that the company's leaders began by explaining the *why* and the *what* of the transformation to all employees. Mobile and digital technologies were dramatically altering the market, they told everybody, and if ING wanted to meet the expectations of customers, improve operations, and deploy new technological capabilities, it would have to become faster, leaner, and more flexible. To do that, they said, the company planned to make investments that would reduce costs and improve service. But it would also eliminate a significant number of jobs—at least a quarter of the total workforce.

Then came the *how*. Rather than letting the ax fall on select employees—a process that creates psychological trauma throughout a company—ING decided that almost everybody at the company, regardless of tenure or seniority, would be required to resign. After that, anybody who felt their attitude, capabilities, and skills would be a good fit at the "new" bank could apply to be rehired. That included Van den Boogert himself. Employees who did not get rehired would be supported by a program that would help them find jobs outside ING.

None of this made the company's transformation easy, of course. But according to Van den Boogert, the inclusive approach adopted by management significantly minimized the pain that employees felt during the transition, and it immediately set the new, smaller bank on the path to success. The employees who rejoined ING actively embraced its new mission, felt less survivor's remorse, and devoted themselves with excitement to the job of transformation. "When you talk about the *why*, *what*, and *how* at the same time," Van den Boogert told us, "people are going to challenge the *why* to prevent the *how*. But in this case, everyone had already been inspired by the *why* and *what*."

3. Look beyond the "spot market" for talent

Most successful companies have adopted increasingly aggressive strategies for finding critical high-skilled talent. Now they must expand that approach to include a wider range of employees. AT&T recognized that need in 2013, while developing its Workforce 2020 strategy, which focused on how the company would make the transition from a hardware-centric to a software-centric network.

The company had undergone a major transformation once before, in 1917, when it launched plans to use mechanical switchboards rather than human operators. But it carried that transformation out over the course of five decades! The Workforce 2020 transformation was much more complex and had to happen on a much faster timeline.

To get started, AT&T undertook a systematic audit of its quarter of a million employees to catalog their current skills and compare those with the skills it expected to need during and after its revamp. Ultimately, the company identified 100,000 employees whose jobs were likely to disappear, and several areas in which it would face skills and competency shortages. Armed with those insights, the company launched an ambitious, multiyear $1 billion initiative to develop an internal talent pipeline instead of simply playing the "spot market" for talent. In short, to meet its evolving needs, AT&T decided to make retraining available to its existing workforce. Since then, its employees have taken nearly 3 million online courses designed to help them acquire skills for new jobs in fields such as application development and cloud computing.

Already, this effort has yielded some unexpected benefits. The company now hires far fewer contractors to meet its needs for technical skills, for example. "We're shifting to employees," one of the company's top executives told CNBC this past March, "because we're starting to see the talent inside."

4. Collaborate to deepen the talent pool

In a fast-evolving environment, competing for talent doesn't work. It simply leads to a tragedy of the commons. Individual companies try to grab the biggest share of the skilled labor available, and these self-interested attempts just end up creating a shortage for all.

To avoid that problem, companies will have to fundamentally change their outlook and work together to ensure that the talent pool is constantly refreshed and updated. That will mean teaming up with other companies in the same industry or region to identify relevant skills, invest in developing curricula, and provide on-the-job training. It will also require forging new relationships for developing talent by, for instance, engaging with entrepreneurs and technology developers, partnering with educational institutions, and collaborating with policymakers.

U.S. utilities companies have already begun doing this. In 2006 they joined forces to establish the Center for Energy Workforce Development (CEWD). The mission of the center, which has no physical office and is staffed primarily by former employees from member companies, is to figure out what jobs and skills the industry will need most as its older workers retire—and then how best to create a pipeline to meet those needs. "We're used to working together in this industry," Ann Randazzo, the center's executive director, told us. "When there's a storm, everybody gets in their trucks. Even if we compete in certain areas, including for workers, we've all got to work together to build this pipeline, or there just aren't going to be enough people."

The center quickly determined that three of the industry's most critical middle-skills jobs—linemen, field operators, and energy technicians—would be hit hard by the retirement of workers in the near future. Together, those three jobs make up almost 40% of a typical utility's workforce. To make sure they wouldn't go unfilled, CEWD implemented a two-pronged strategy. It created detailed tool kits, curricula, and training materials for all three jobs, which it made available free to utility companies; and it launched a grassroots movement to reach out to next-generation workers and promote careers in the industry.

CEWD believes in connecting with promising talent early—very early. To that end, it has been working with hundreds of elementary, middle, and high schools to create materials and programs that introduce students to the benefits of working in the industry. These include a sense of larger purpose (delivering critical services to customers); stability (no offshoring of jobs, little technological displacement); the use of automation and technology to make jobs less physically taxing and more intellectually engaging; and, last but not least, surprisingly high wages. Describing the program to us, Randazzo said, "You're *growing* a workforce. We had to start from scratch to get students in the lower grades to understand what they need to do and to really be able to grow that all the way through high school to community colleges and universities. And it's not a one-and-done. We have to continually nurture it."

5. Find ways to manage chronic uncertainty

In today's world, managers know that if they don't swiftly identify and respond to shifts, their companies will be left behind. So how can firms best prepare?

The office-furniture manufacturer Steelcase has come up with some intriguing ideas. One is its Strategic Workforce Architecture and Transformation (SWAT) team, which tracks emerging trends and conducts real-time experiments in how to respond to them. The team has launched an internal platform called Loop, for example, where employees can volunteer to work on projects outside their own functions. This benefits both the company and its employees: As new needs arise, the company can quickly locate workers within its ranks who have the motivation and skills to meet them, and workers can gain experience and develop new capabilities in ways that their current jobs simply don't allow.

Employees at Steelcase have embraced Loop, and its success illustrates an idea that came through very clearly in our survey results. As Jill Dark, the director of the SWAT team, put it to us, "If you give people the opportunity to learn something new or to show their craft, they will give you their best work. The magic is in providing the opportunity."

That's a lesson that all managers should heed.

Originally published in May–June 2019. Reprint R1903H

Discussion Guide

Are you feeling inspired by what you've read in this collection? Do you want to share the ideas in the articles or explore the insights you've gleaned with others? This discussion guide offers an opportunity to dig a little deeper, with questions to prompt personal reflection and to start conversations with your team.

You don't need to have read the book from beginning to end to use this guide. Choose the questions that apply to the articles you have read or that you feel might spark the liveliest discussion.

Reflect on key takeaways from your reading to help you adopt the ideas and techniques you want to integrate into your work as a leader. What tools can you share with your team to help everyone be their best? Becoming the leader you want to be starts with a detailed plan—and a commitment to carrying it out.

1. When your organization has undertaken change efforts in the past, what kinds of challenges has it run into? How did leadership respond to them effectively—or ineffectively? What could your company do to address those barriers for future change initiatives?

2. Does your organization treat transformation as a continuous process or a onetime event? What are some examples of how that happens? What could the company do to better integrate change and adaptation into its operating rhythms?

3. Think about the major factors that have contributed to your organization's success in the past. What strategies, processes, or practices have played an important role? What dynamics in your industry might make those factors less effective in the future?

4. When has your organization missed out on a new opportunity because decision-makers wanted too much information about it before acting? What were the consequences? How could your company adjust its decision-making processes to move faster when opportunities arise?

5. When leaders are announcing or rolling out a reorganization, what mistakes have you seen them make? What effects did those mistakes have? What could your company's leaders do to make the next reorganization smoother?

6. How does your company involve employees in the planning and decision-making process of organizational change? How could leaders involve them more effectively? Are certain teams or individuals particularly important to engage first?

7. Take a few minutes and think about how you would tell your company's long-term narrative. How would you summarize where it has been and where it's going? When your organization is planning for the future, what aspects of its culture or norms are important to honor?

8. Think of a recent change initiative at your company. What strategies did leaders use to communicate its purpose and benefits to employees? How could they better tailor that message to the needs and priorities of your team?

9. Who are the key influencers in your company that others turn to for advice and information? What makes them so influential? How could you and your team better engage them in your future change efforts?

10. What strategies have you used, or seen company leaders use, to manage resistance to change? What made those strategies work well, or not?

11. When have you had to balance competing priorities during an organizational change? How did you navigate those situations? How could you do it more effectively next time?

12. What actions do you or company leaders take to create a learning culture? What could decision-makers do to better support employees' eagerness to learn new skills over time?

13. What other sources on change management have had a significant impact on your work? Were there voices or subtopics you missed in this collection? Were there voices or subtopics included that surprised you?

14. After reading and reflecting on this book and discussing it with people on your team, write down the ideas and techniques you want to try. Think of how you might experiment and implement them in both the short term and long term. Draft a plan to move forward.

About the Contributors

N. Anand is the Shell Professor of Global Leadership and the dean of research at IMD.

Scott D. Anthony is a clinical professor at Dartmouth College's Tuck School of Business, a senior partner at Innosight, and the lead author of *Eat, Sleep, Innovate* (Harvard Business Review Press, 2020) and *Dual Transformation* (Harvard Business Review Press, 2017).

Jean-Louis Barsoux is a term research professor at IMD and a coauthor of *ALIEN Thinking: The Unconventional Path to Breakthrough Ideas*.

Julie Battilana is the Joseph C. Wilson Professor of Business Administration at Harvard Business School and the Alan L. Gleitsman Professor of Social Innovation at Harvard Kennedy School, where she is the founder and faculty chair of the Social Innovation and Change Initiative. She is a coauthor of *Power, for All*.

Utsav Bhatt is an associate partner at Innosight.

Tiziana Casciaro is a professor of organizational behavior and HR management and holds the Marcel Desautels Chair in Integrative Thinking at the University of Toronto's Rotman School of Management. She is a coauthor of *Power, for All*.

About the Contributors

Alice de Chalendar is a consultant at Boston Consulting Group and a researcher at the BCG Henderson Institute.

Frances X. Frei is the UPS Foundation Professor of Service Management at Harvard Business School and is a coauthor of the books *Move Fast and Fix Things* (Harvard Business Review Press, 2023) and *Unleashed* (Harvard Business Review Press, 2020).

Joseph Fuller is a professor of management practice and a faculty cochair of the Project on Managing the Future of Work at Harvard Business School.

Vijay Govindarajan is the Coxe Distinguished Professor at Dartmouth College's Tuck School of Business, a Dartmouth-wide chair and the highest distinction awarded to Dartmouth faculty; a faculty partner in the Silicon Valley incubator Mach49; and senior adviser at the strategy consulting firm Acropolis Advisors. He is a *New York Times* and *Wall Street Journal* bestselling author. His latest book is *Fusion Strategy* (Harvard Business Review Press, 2024). Two of his HBR articles won McKinsey Awards for best article published in the magazine, and two others are HBR all-time top 50 bestsellers.

Stephen Heidari-Robinson is the managing director of Quartz Associates (a consulting and software company that delivers organizational change), a visiting fellow at Oxford University, a coauthor of *ReOrg: How to Get It Right* (Harvard Business Review Press, 2016), and a contributor to *HBR's 10 Must Reads on Managing in a Downturn*.

Ronald Heifetz is the founder of the Center for Public Leadership at Harvard Kennedy School and a coauthor of *The Practice* of *Adaptive Leadership* (Harvard Business Press, 2009) and the bestselling *Leadership on the Line* (Harvard Business Review Press, 2017).

Suzanne Heywood is the chair of Quartz Associates, managing director of Exor, chair and acting CEO of CNHI, a coauthor of *ReOrg: How to Get It Right* (Harvard Business Review Press, 2016), and a contributor to *HBR's 10 Must Reads on Managing in a Downturn* (Harvard Business Review Press, 2020).

Robert Kegan is the William and Miriam Meehan Professor of Adult Learning and Professional Development at the Harvard Graduate School of Education.

John P. Kotter is a bestselling author, award-winning business and management thought leader, and business entrepreneur, and the Konosuke Matsushita Professor of Leadership, Emeritus, at Harvard Business School. His ideas, books, and company, Kotter, help people lead organizations in an era of increasingly rapid change. He is a coauthor of the book *Change*, which details how leaders can leverage challenges and opportunities to make sustainable workplace changes in a rapidly accelerating world.

Lisa Lahey is a lecturer at the Harvard Graduate School of Education and the cofounder of the consultancy Minds at Work.

Marty Linsky is a member of the Kennedy School faculty at Harvard Business School and a coauthor of *The Practice of Adaptive Leadership* (Harvard Business Press, 2009) and the bestselling *Leadership on the Line* (Harvard Business Review Press, 2017).

About the Contributors

Patrick Litre leads Bain's Global Transformation and Change practice and is a partner based in Atlanta.

Michael Mankins is a leader in Bain's Organization and Strategy practices and is a partner based in Austin, Texas. He is a coauthor of *Time, Talent, Energy* (Harvard Business Review Press, 2017).

Anne Morriss is an entrepreneur and the executive founder of the Leadership Consortium. She is also the coauthor of *Move Fast and Fix Things* (Harvard Business Review Press, 2023) and *Unleashed* (Harvard Business Review Press, 2020).

Antonio Nieto-Rodriguez is the author of the *Harvard Business Review Project Management Handbook,* five other books, and the HBR article "The Project Economy Has Arrived." His research and global impact on modern management have been recognized by Thinkers50. A pioneer and leading authority in teaching and advising executives on the art and science of strategy implementation and modern project management, Nieto-Rodriguez is a visiting professor at seven leading business schools, the founder of Projects & Company, and a cofounder of the Strategy Implementation Institute and PMOtto.

Andrea Belk Olson is a differentiation strategist, speaker, author, and customer-centricity expert. She is the CEO of Pragmadik, a behavioral science–driven change agency, and has served as an outside consultant for EY and McKinsey. She is the author of three books, a four-time ADDY award winner, and a contributing author for *Entrepreneur* magazine, *Rotman Management Magazine, Chief Executive,* and *Customer Experience Magazine.*

Manjari Raman is a senior program director and a senior researcher for Harvard Business School's U.S. Competitiveness Project and the Project on Managing the Future of Work.

Pontus M. A. Siren is a partner at Innosight.

Judith K. Wallenstein is a senior partner and managing director at Boston Consulting Group, a BCG Fellow, and the director of the BCG Henderson Institute in Europe.

Index

Acer, 126–127
adaptability of workforce, 179–192
   employee development programs, 186–192
   forces of disruption, 181–186
adaptive change, 136, 138
Adobe, 27–29
Ambition 2030 plan, 94
Amgen, 31–32
Anand, N., 115–133
anger, 85
Anthony, Scott D., 41–53
artificial intelligence, 184–185
aspirational thinking, 27–29
assumptions. *See* big assumptions
AT&T, 32, 33, 189–190
attainability of change, 70
authenticity behind change, 70
automation, 184–185

Bain & Company, 20, 23, 30
Barsoux, Jean-Louis, 115–133
Battilana, Julie, 101–114
behavior
   communication via, 11–12
   supporting change via, 70, 142–144
benchmarks, aspirational thinking versus, 27–29
benefits cards, 94–98
benefits-driven transformation, 93–99
Bezos, Jeff, 80
Bhatt, Utsav, 41–53
big assumptions
   identifying, 171–174
   questioning, 174–177
   testing, 176

big-picture perspective, 140–141
Bradway, Bob, 31–32
bridging networks, 106–110, 114
Browne, John, 61
"burning platforms," 41
Burns, Ursula, 81
business plan review (BPR) process, 24–25

capital investment in transformation programs, 32–33
Carlzon, Jan, 82
Carrefour, 129
Casciaro, Tiziana, 101–114
catalysts for change, 118–120
Center for Energy Workforce Development (CEWD), 190–191
centrality (in informal network), 103–106, 114
change, resistance to. *See* resistance to change
change agent networks, 101–114
   determining type of, 110
   fence-sitters and resisters, 110–114
   informal network centrality, 103–106, 114
   shape of network, 106–110
change management
   employee buy-in, 67–71
   failure rate of projects, 90, 115
   growth rate of projects, 89–90
   mediocrity in outcomes, 21–22
   proactive versus reactive, 41–53
   success rate, 19–22, 30
   See also leadership; reorganizations; transformation

change management, errors in, 1–18, 20–21
  guiding coalition, ineffective, 7–8
  institutionalizing change, failure of, 17–18
  premature victory declaration, 15–17
  prioritizing changes, 115–118, 127–129
  in reorganizations, 59
  sense of urgency, lack of, 2–6
  short-term wins, lack of, 14–15
  vision, lack of, 8–10
  vision, obstacles to, 12–14
  vision, undercommunicating, 10–12
change management, keys to success, 22–34
  aspirational thinking, 27–29
  continuous process, transformation as, 22–24
  external capital investment, 32–33
  institutionalizing change, 24–25
  managing organizational energy, 25–27
  middle-out approach, 29–32
change management, stages of, 4–5
  guiding coalition, 7–8
  institutionalizing change, 17–18
  sense of urgency, 2–6
  short-term wins, 14–15
  vision, communicating, 10–12
  vision, creating, 8–10
  vision, removing obstacles from, 12–14
Chicago Bulls, 148–150
Christensen, Clayton, 44, 49
chronic uncertainty, managing, 191–192
Clinton, Bill, 155–156
cloud-based software, 27–29
cohesive networks, 106–110, 114
collaboration on talent pool, 190–191

communication
  of prioritization choices, 132–133
  in proactive change management, 51–52
  in reorganizations, 61
  of vision, 10–12
  See also storytelling
competing commitments, 159–178
  group dynamics and, 165–166
  identifying big assumptions, 171–174
  in managers, 177–178
  questioning big assumptions, 174–177
  uncovering, 166–171
confidants, need for, 154
conflict management, 145–147
continuous process, transformation as, 22–24
control, need for, 151–152
core rigidities, 130
Cosentino, 131
Covid-19, 86–87
Cox, Berkeley, 42, 45–46, 50–51
crises, manufacturing, 6
criticism of leadership, 154–156
culture (of organization), institutionalizing change in, 17–18
customer focus, 120, 121, 124

Dark, Jill, 192
debating priorities, 130–131
de Chalendar, Alice, 179–192
dedicated teams, 39
delegating responsibility, 148–150
Dell, Michael, 23, 32
Dell Agenda, 23–24
Dell Technologies, 23–24, 32
dependency (on leadership), 152–153
devotion, 84
Digital Equipment Corporation, 153
digital transformation benefits card, 94–98

discipline, 119
discomfort, 85
disruption, forces of, 181–186
disruptive innovation model, 49
divergent changes, 107, 111–113
Domino's, 78–79, 82
Doyle, Patrick, 78–79

Ellison, Marvin, 116–117
Emerging Business Opportunities (EBO) process, 39
emotions in storytelling, 84–87
employee adaptability. *See* adaptability of workforce
employee buy-in, 67–71, 187–188
employee resistance. *See* resistance to change
energy (of organization), managing, 25–27
engaging employees in transformation, 187–188
English, Paul, 84
enthusiasm, 84
errors in change management. *See* change management, errors in
Expeditors, 187
external capital investment in transformation programs, 32–33

Facebook, 77–78
failure, reasons for. *See* change management, errors in
failure rate of projects, 90, 115
fellowship, 85
fence-sitters (uncommitted), 110–114, 141–142
Ferraro, John, 55
Ford Motor Company, 24–25, 32, 83
forgetting the past, 35–40
formal hierarchy, informal network versus, 104

Frei, Frances X., 73–87
frustration, 84
Fuller, Joseph, 179–192

gatekeepers, 76
Gates, Bill, 153
gig economy, 184
global presence, 120, 121, 124
Goleman, Daniel, 86
Govindarajan, Vijay, 35–40
grace, 85
gratitude, 86
group dynamics, 165–166
GroupM, 132
growth rate of projects, 89–90
guiding coalition, creating, 7–8

Haiman, Bob, 143
happiness, 84–85
Hart, Gary, 155
Haugen, Frances, 77–78
Heidari-Robinson, Stephen, 55–65
Heifetz, Ronald, 135–157
Heywood, Suzanne, 55–65
Hoffman, Bryce, 83
Home Depot, 128
Hrdlicka, Jayne, 26–27
Hsieh, Tony, 84
HubSpot, 85

IBM, 38–39, 126, 153
immunity to change. *See* resistance to change
impartiality, 71
importance, feeling of, 152–153
incentives, 38
informal influencers, 68
informal network centrality, 103–106, 114
information-action paradox, 42–45, 48–49

Infosys, 128
ING Netherlands, 187–188
innovation, 120, 121, 124
institutionalizing change, 17–18, 24–25
Intuit, 46
iPhone, 33

Jackson, Phil, 148–150
J.C. Penney (JCP), 116–117, 128
Jobs, Steve, 92
Johnson, Ron, 116–117, 128
Jordan, Michael, 148–150
joy, 85

Kanter, Rosabeth Moss, 78
Kanter's Law, 78
Karvinen, Jouko, 125
Kayak, 84
Kegan, Robert, 159–178
Kerr, Steve, 85
Khosrowshahi, Dara, 76–77
Kneeland, Mike, 38
Knudstorp, Jørgen Vig, 119, 133
Kotter, John P., 1–18, 20
Kukoc, Toni, 148–149
KWM (King & Wood Mallesons) Australia, 42, 45–53
    information-action paradox at, 45–47, 48–49
    private data, generating, 47–48
    proactive change management, impact of, 50–53
    structured discussions at, 49–50
    threshold of proof, lowering, 48–50

Lahey, Lisa, 159–178
latent change, 69
leadership
    adaptive versus technical change, 136, 138
    behavior, supporting change via, 142–144
    benefits of, 156–157
    communication of choices, 132–133
    confidants, need for, 154
    conflict management, 145–147
    control, need for, 151–152
    delegating responsibility, 148–150
    developing, 125–127
    forces of disruption, 181–186
    importance, feeling of, 152–153
    management versus, 3–4
    participation versus observation, 140–141
    personal attacks against, 154–156
    relationships in, 141–142
    respite for, 153–154
    risks of, 135–137
    self-destructive tendencies, 150–156
learning culture, fostering, 186–187
Legere, John, 32–33, 74
legitimacy, fostering, 68
Lego, 119, 133
Lenovo, 126–127
Leonardi, Paul, 83–84
lessons learned from change management errors, 2
Lewin, Kurt, 22
License Raj system, 36
The Limited, 144
Linsky, Marty, 135–157
Litre, Patrick, 19–34
Loop, 192

Mahindra, Anand, 37–38
Mahindra Group, 36–38
Mahoney, Michelle, 42, 45, 51
management
    competing commitments in, 177–178
    employee development programs, 186–192

forces of disruption, 181–186
  leadership versus, 3–4
  mandate for change, 78–79
Mankins, Michael, 19–34
Mariscal, Marguerite Zabar, 82
McKinstry, Nancy, 64
McNamara, Mark, 51
mediocrity in change management outcomes, 21–22
Meta, 77–78
micro-changes, 70
Microsoft, 29, 153
middle-out approach to change management, 29–32
mistakes in change management. *See* change management, errors in
Momofuku, 82
Morita, Akio, 92
Morriss, Anne, 73–87
Mulally, Alan, 24–25, 32, 83
Musk, Elon, 61
Myers, Pete, 149

Narayen, Shantanu, 28, 29
Nardelli, Bob, 128
narratives. *See* storytelling
National Health Service (NHS), 101–102, 107–109, 113, 114
Neeley, Tsedal, 83
networks (of change agents), 101–114
  determining type of, 110
  fence-sitters and resisters, 110–114
  informal network centrality, 103–106, 114
  shape of network, 106–110
neutral change facilitation, 71
New York Knicks, 148, 149
Nieto-Rodriguez, Antonio, 89–99
nimbleness, 120, 122, 124
nondivergent changes, 107–108, 111–112

Nooyi, Indra, 86
Norske Skog, 118

O'Brien, Tim, 73
observation, participation versus, 140–141
off-site retreats, 8
Olofsson, Lars, 129
Olsen, Ken, 153
Olson, Andrea Belk, 67–71
One Ford, 24–25, 83
optimism in storytelling, 80–81
organizational culture, institutionalizing change in, 17–18
organizational energy, managing, 25–27
Ørsted, 80
ownership (of change), 68

participation, observation versus, 140–141
past history (of company), honoring, 75–78
past mindsets, letting go of, 35–40
Pathfinders program, 125–126
Patterson, Gene, 142–143
perception gap, 179–192
  forces of disruption, 181–186
  solutions for overcoming, 186–192
personal attacks against leadership, 154–156
Pippen, Scottie, 148–150
Pizza Turnaround, 79
Plassat, Georges, 129
portfolio reconfiguration, 39
Poulsen, Henrik, 80
"practice what you preach," 142–143
premature victory declaration, 15–17
primal leadership, 86
prioritizing changes
  choosing direction via quests, 120–125
  communication of choices, 132–133

prioritizing changes (*continued*)
  debating priorities, 130–131
  errors in, 115–118, 127–129
  leadership development, 125–127
  pursuit of value, 118–120
  quest audits, 124–125, 129–130
private data, 42, 47–48
proactive change management, 41–53
  impact of, 50–53
  information-action paradox, 42–45
  private data, generating, 47–48
  threshold of proof, lowering, 48–50
Procter & Gamble (P&G), 94
profit and loss statements in reorganizations, 57–58, 60
proprietary models, 47–48
purpose-driven transformations, 90–93
pursuit of value, 118–120

qualitative data, 47
quantitative data, 47
quest audits, 124–125, 129–130
questioning big assumptions, 174–177
quests
  choosing direction via, 120–125
  errors in, 127–129
  leadership development in, 124–127

Raman, Manjari, 179–192
Randazzo, Ann, 190–191
reactive change management, 41
regret, 84
relationships in leadership, 141–142
relevance (of change), 69
reorganizations, 55–65
  communication in, 61
  course corrections in, 64–65
  current strengths and weaknesses, evaluating, 58–60

  details of, managing, 63–64
  failure, reasons for, 59
  multiple options, considering, 60p, 62
  profit and loss statement, developing, 57–58, 60
repetition in storytelling, 82–86
resistance to change, 159–178
  group dynamics and, 165–166
  identifying big assumptions, 171–174
  in managers, 177–178
  questioning big assumptions, 174–177
  uncovering competing commitments, 166–171
resisters, 110–114
responsibility (for problems)
  acknowledging, 143–144
  delegating, 148–150
rigor in storytelling, 80–81
Riot Games, 77, 78
risks of leadership, 135–137
Rometty, Ginni, 85
Roosevelt, Franklin, 142, 147

Scandinavian Airlines (SAS), 82
self-awareness, 87
self-destructive tendencies of leadership, 150–156
self-importance, 152–153
self-protection, 171
sense of urgency, lack of, 2–6
Shah, Dharmesh, 85
shape (of network), 106–110
short-term wins, 14–15
Siren, Pontus M. A., 41–53
skills, demand for, 182
SMART purposes, 93
Sony, 92
"spot market" talent, 189–190
stages of change management. *See* change management, stages of
Steelcase, 192

Stora Enso, 119, 122–123, 125–126
storytelling, 73–87
   combining elements into narrative, 81–82
   emotions in, 84–87
   honoring past, 75–78
   mandate for change, 78–79
   repetition in, 82–86
   rigor and optimism in, 80–81
   simple descriptions, 74–75
St. Petersburg Times, 142–143
Strategic Workforce Architecture and Transformation (SWAT), 192
strengths and weaknesses, evaluating, 58–60
structured discussions, 49–50
success rate of transformation programs, 19–22, 30
sustainability, 94, 120, 122–123, 125

talent pipeline, 189–191
technical change, 136, 138
technological disruption, 182, 184–185
testing big assumptions, 176
threshold of proof, lowering, 48–50
T-Mobile, 32–33, 74
training programs, 186–187, 189–191
transformation
   as benefits-driven, 93–99
   catalysts for change, 118–120
   choosing direction via quests, 120–125
   communication of choices, 132–133
   as continuous process, 22–24
   debating priorities, 130–131
   engaging employees in, 187–188
   external capital investment in, 32–33
   leadership development, 125–127
   prioritizing changes, errors in, 115–118, 127–129
   as purpose-driven, 90–93
   quest audits, 124–125, 129–130
   See also change management

Uber, 76–77
uncommitted (fence-sitters), 110–114, 141–142
"unfreeze-change-refreeze" model, 23
United Rentals, 38, 39
unlearning the past, 35–40
utility companies, 190–191

value generation, 118–120
Van den Boogert, Vincent, 187–188
Verizon, 32, 33
victory declaration, premature, 15–17
Virgin Australia, 26–27
vision
   combining elements into narrative, 81–82
   lack of, 8–10
   obstacles to, 12–14
   undercommunicating, 10–12

Wallenstein, Judith K., 179–192
Weiner, Russell, 79
Wexner, Leslie, 144
Workforce 2020 strategy, 189–190
workforce adaptability. *See* adaptability of workforce
work models, changes in, 183
worldviews, 172–173

Xerox, 81

Yang Yuanqing, 127

Zappos, 84

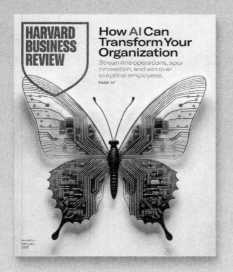

Work is hard. Let us help.

Engage with HBR content the way you want, on any device.

Whether you run an organization, a team, or you're trying to change the trajectory of your own career, let *Harvard Business Review* be your guide. Level up your leadership skills by subscribing to HBR.

HBR is more than just a magazine—it's access to a world of business insights through articles, videos, audio content, charts, ebooks, case studies, and more.

SUBSCRIBE TODAY
hbr.org/subscriptions